Positive Psychology
Arts Activities

of related interest

Creative DBT Activities Using Music and Arts
Interventions for Enhancing Engagement and Effectiveness in Therapy
Deborah Spiegel with Suzanne Makary and Lauren Bonavitacola
ISBN 978 1 78775 180 4
eISBN 978 1 78775 182 8

Quick and Creative Art Projects for Creative
Therapists with (Very) Limited Budgets
Rachel Brandoff and Angel Thompson
ISBN 978 1 78592 794 2
eISBN 978 1 78450 787 9

Therapeutic Photography
Enhancing Self-Esteem, Self-Efficacy and Resilience
Neil Gibson
ISBN 978 1 78592 155 1
eISBN 978 1 78450 421 2

The Handbook of Art Therapy and Digital Technology
Edited by Cathy Malchiodi, PhD
Foreword by Dr Val Huet
ISBN 978 1 78592 792 8
eISBN 978 1 78450 774 9

Positive Psychology Arts Activities

Creative Tools for Therapeutic Practice and Supervision

OLENA DAREWYCH

Foreword by
James O. Pawelski and Louis Tay

Jessica Kingsley Publishers
London and Philadelphia

Table 4.1 reproduced with kind permission of VIA Institute of Character
Appendix D image reproduced with kind permission of Erin Hunt Rado
Appendix images J, O and R reproduced with kind permission of Michael Kuzmich
Appendix P and Q reproduced with kind permission of Esther Zeller Cooper

First published in 2020
by Jessica Kingsley Publishers
73 Collier Street
London N1 9BE, UK
and
400 Market Street, Suite 400
Philadelphia, PA 19106, USA

www.jkp.com

Copyright © Olena Darewych 2020
Foreword copyright © James O. Pawelski and Louis Tay 2020

Front cover image source: Nesting doll image by Olena Darewych.

Library of Congress Cataloging in Publication Data
A CIP catalog record for this book is available from the Library of Congress

British Library Cataloguing in Publication Data
A CIP catalogue record for this book is available from the British Library

ISBN 978 1 78592 836 9
eISBN 978 1 78450 986 6

Printed and bound in Great Britain

Contents

List of Figures and Tables

Figures

Tables

Foreword

When Martin Seligman, Mihaly Csikszentmihalyi, and their colleagues launched positive psychology, their aim was to encourage the scientific study and evidence-based practice of what we value most in life. That is, their goal was a balanced consideration not just of the obstacles to human flourishing but also of the factors that actually lead to it. Although it is easy to focus our attention on the study and mitigation of what is *not* going well, they argued, it is just as important to understand and cultivate what *is* going well.

When we began working on the arts, humanities, and human flourishing, our aim was to encourage a collaborative approach to understanding how art, music, movies, literature, theatre, history, philosophy, religion, and similar domains can aid in the conceptualization and cultivation of well-being. Finding that much of the academic study in these disciplines was focused on what is not going well in our lives and in our world, we argued that it is just as important to understand and cultivate what *is* going well. This involves both the study of these disciplines, and the practice of the art forms underlying so many of them. Although individuals seek out art, music, drama, and dance therapies because of the things that are not going well in their lives, a human flourishing approach to the arts and humanities reminds us not to lose sight of the gratitude, optimism, character strengths, relationships, meaning, and other factors that can help relieve pathology and reconnect us with what makes life worth living.

In this book, Dr. Olena Darewych builds on the fundamental insight in positive psychology that we are extending to the arts and humanities: human flourishing is as much about the cultivation of well-being as it is about the mitigation of ill-being. It is as much about the direct fostering of positive factors as it is about the overcoming of the negative factors that stand in our way. Even in therapeutic contexts—or perhaps *especially* in therapeutic contexts—it is important to balance a consideration of the obstacles to human flourishing with an emphasis on what promotes it. In our conceptual work, we have proposed that arts activities have the power to unlock well-being by allowing us to immerse ourselves in aesthetic experience, engage in reflection, acquire new skills, create connections with others, and generate new ways of expressing ourselves.

We recommend this book as a powerful, practical companion for anyone interested in the integration of positive psychology and the arts in therapeutic contexts. It contains concise introductions to key domains in positive psychology, including creativity, flow, positive emotions, character strengths, self-awareness, goals, meaning, spirituality, and well-being. Each domain is accompanied by a variety of simple but profound artistic activities, along with guidance on how to use them most effectively. Engagement in these activities can help individuals directly cultivate these positive domains and also explore and clarify obstacles that are holding them back. These activities may be particularly useful in situations where it is important to complement or replace the writing-based approach of many traditional positive psychology interventions.

We welcome this book with its treasure trove of activities, as we believe they can help individuals decrease their ill-being and increase their well-being. We also believe they can help in the further development and scientific testing of these and similar interventions, leading to an increase in our empirical understanding of how the arts and humanities can support human flourishing across a variety of contexts. In the meantime, we express our deep appreciation and respect for each mental health practitioner who reads this book: we are grateful for your dedication to mental health, and we wish you every success as you incorporate the ideas and activities in this book into your practice.

James O. Pawelski
Director of the Humanities and Human Flourishing Project,
University of Pennsylvania, Philadelphia, PA

Louis Tay
Co-Director of the Humanities and Human Flourishing Project,
Purdue University, West Lafayette, IN

Acknowledgements

I thank my clients and students who enabled me throughout the years to apply the positive psychology arts activities presented in this book in clinical, educational, and supervisory settings. A special thanks to those clients and students who generously gave permission to use their de-identified artwork in this book.

I thank my colleagues Esther Zeller Cooper, Sajel Bellon, Kerri Brock, Dan Tomasulo, Ryan Niemiec, Judy Rubin, Duanita Eleniak, Barbara Collins, Rebecca Wilkinson, Gioia Chilton, and Erin Rado for their encouragement and helpful discussions on the interplay of positive psychology and the arts during the writing of this book.

I thank Jane Evans of Jessica Kingsley Publishers for her invitation to write this book.

Special thanks go to Michael Kuzmich for creating a number of the arts activity sheets presented in the appendix section of this book and his willingness to share his personal creative activity—that of digital design—with mental health professionals.

And finally, I thank my husband and children for filling my heart with love, my soul with zest, and my life with meaning on a daily basis. With deep gratitude.

Preface

This book presents action-oriented and reflective arts activities that creatively and playfully bring positive psychology concepts such as character strengths, flow, goals, meaning, and spirituality to life. The positive psychology arts activities described in this book can be administered by mental health professionals for their clients who are physically, psychologically, and socially prepared to creatively and metaphorically identify their character strengths, awaken positive emotions within themselves, nurture meaningful relationships, undergo forward movement along their life journey, and shine light on some of the positives in their lives. This particular how-to book is an assemblage of arts activities that I have designed along my professional journey as a clinician-educator-researcher-supervisor, as well as those formulated by my colleagues from the fields of creative arts therapies and positive psychology: Erin Rado, Cathy Malchiodi, Ryan Niemiec, Michael Steger, Dan Tomasulo, Esther Zeller Cooper, and Martin Seligman. The step-by-step instructions for each activity are straightforward and the threshold for creativity, time, and effort is quite low. It is important for mental health professionals to adapt these arts activities to suit their clients' emotional and physical states, developmental age, preferred art forms, and cultural experiences. I describe throughout the book how particular positive arts activities can be modified in supervisory sessions for supervisees to identify their character strengths and competencies, and used as resources to bring about positive change in their lives.

I hope mental health professionals such as creative arts therapists, psychotherapists, and psychologists who are passionate about human flourishing will find these positive psychology arts activities invaluable tools for cultivating their clients' mental health and well-being as well as their own.

INTRODUCTION

Positive psychology

Positive psychology, also known as the science of well-being, is the study of human flourishing and optimal functioning of communities and organizations. The idea of positive psychology was initiated in 1998 by psychologist Martin Seligman during his Presidential Address to the American Psychological Association (APA) (Seligman, 1999). At the time, the discipline of psychology was based on the disease model and human illnesses; therefore, Seligman's mission was to help "build the scientific infrastructure of a field that would investigate what makes life worth living: positive emotions, positive character, and positive institutions" (Seligman, 2004, p.xi). As a result, positive psychology's contemporary theoretical framework devotes greater attention to individuals' positive human qualities as growth, resiliency, strengths, and well-being, rather than their psychological crises or deficits (Seligman & Csikszentmihályi, 2000). Although a relatively new branch of psychology, its theoretical underpinnings are Rogers's (1951) person-centered therapy, Jahoda's (1958) framework on positive mental health, Maslow's (1970) self-actualization theory, and Frankl's (1986) logotherapy. To this day, scholars and researchers in the field of positive psychology have been examining a variety of topics related to human flourishing, but not limited to: creativity, flow, positive emotions, character strengths, self-awareness, goals, meaning in life, spirituality, and well-being.

In the early stage of the history of positive psychology, there was criticism of the discipline for placing greater emphasis on the positive functioning of people, groups, communities, and organizations (Lazarus, 2003). While this may have been the case, positive psychology's current framework presents a more balanced approach to both the positive and the negative qualities of human and organizational functioning (Joseph, 2015).

Since the inception of positive psychology, a number of subfields have developed, for example positive education (Seligman *et al.*, 2009), positive supervision (Bannink, 2015), positive therapy (Joseph & Linley, 2004), and positive psychotherapy (Rashid, 2008).

Positive psychotherapy

The applications of positive psychology in clinical settings continue to grow. During a therapeutic session, the role of the mental health professional is not just to alleviate distress in their clients, but also to promote their physical, psychological, social, and spiritual well-being. Positive psychotherapy's therapeutic approach involves clients undergoing various exercises over three stages. First, clients identify their character strengths and then build on these, often by means of homework assignments. During the second stage, clients work through unresolved conflicts, explore the triggers of their negative emotions, and engage in interventions that evoke positive emotions. During the final stage, clients focus on establishing positive relationships and sources that make their life feel meaningful (Rashid, 2015). To date, the majority of applied positive psychological activities have been designed for adolescents and adults, and typically involve a writing process such as writing a gratitude letter, journaling about their accomplishments, and listing character strengths.

Positive arts

In recent years, additional positive psychology subfields such as positive art (Lomas, 2016), positive art therapy (Chilton & Wilkinson, 2016), and positive arts and humanities (Shim *et al.*, 2019; Tay, Pawelski, & Keith, 2017) have evolved. Scholars and researchers in the subfield of positive arts have commenced exploring the intersectionality between positive psychology and the arts, and how the two approaches, in combination, can enhance individuals' mental health and wellness in clinical, community, and educational settings (Conner, DeYoung, & Silvia, 2016; Darewych, 2014; Forgeard & Eichner, 2014; Kurtz & Lyubomirsky, 2013; Lomas, 2016; Wilkinson & Chilton, 2013).

Historically, the arts such as dance, drama, music, poetry, and storytelling have been used by humans as healing practices, forms of self-expression, and pathways towards self-discovery and transformation. For example, the Egyptians and Greeks used drama and music to express their everyday experiences, while the ancient San people in Africa created rock paintings to protect themselves and their animals from evil spirits (Haslam, 1997; Malchiodi, 2007). In the 21st century, the arts continue to play a vital role across cultures and nations in contributing to psychological well-being and human flourishing. As a result, in recent years a number of creative arts therapists (e.g., art therapists, dance/movement therapists, drama therapists, expressive arts therapists, and music therapists) and psychologists from the subfield of positive arts have developed arts activities specifically grounded in positive psychology theoretical underpinnings. These arts activities invite individuals in clinical and non-clinical settings to creatively express unresolved conflicts and deep emotions in a symbolic manner (Puig *et al.*, 2006), build on character strengths (O'Hanlon & Bertolino, 2012), express gratitude (Tomasulo, 2019), evoke positive emotions (Wilkinson & Chilton, 2018), achieve life's meaning (Steger *et al.*, 2013), explore their best possible selves (Owens & Patterson, 2013), cultivate psychological well-being (Darewych & Riedel Bowers, 2017), and connect with the world around them with all their senses (Malchiodi, 2005). Based on Lyubomirsky and Layous's (2013) positive-activity model, in clinical settings it is important that clients engage with their preferred art activity regularly, be open to exploring a variety of different art forms, and create their artwork in the presence of a clinician who guides and supports them during the creative therapeutic journey.

Aim of the book

This book presents action-oriented and reflective arts activities (Figure I.1) grounded in positive psychology frameworks that mental health professionals (e.g., creative arts therapists, psychologists, psychotherapists, registered nurses, and social workers) can integrate in their therapeutic sessions as creative vehicles by which individuals can explore creative outlets, engage in the act of flow, express negative and positive emotions, identify character strengths, undergo self-awareness, gain insight to personal goals, reflect on sources of life meaning, discover spirituality, and cultivate well-being (Figure I.2), even in the midst of struggle and adversity. Each forthcoming chapter provides 1) a brief overview of a positive psychology concept (i.e., creativity, flow, positive emotions, character strengths, self-awareness, goals, meaning, spirituality, and well-being), 2) arts activities associated with the positive psychology concept, 3) post-activity guiding questions that elicit dialogues between therapist and client, 4) case examples illustrating the therapeutic use of a number of the arts activities, and 5) suggestions on how mental health professionals who provide supervision can adapt a number of these positive psychology arts activities for supervisees to identify their character strengths, competencies, and goals, and utilize them as resources to bring about positive change in their personal lives.

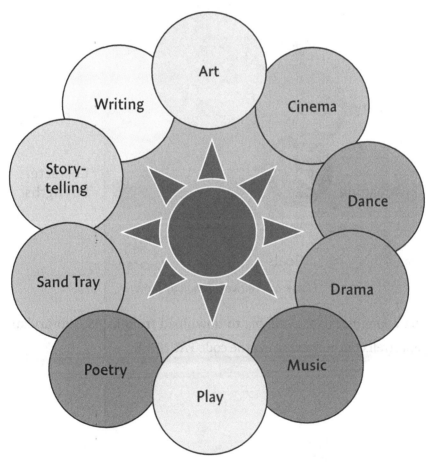

Figure I.1 Positive psychology arts activities

Each symbol represents a positive psychology concept. Each forthcoming chapter provides a brief overview of a positive psychology concept (i.e., creativity, flow, positive emotions, character strengths, self-awareness, goals, meaning, spirituality, and well-being), and arts activities associated with the positive psychology concept.

Figure I.2 Positive psychology concepts

The appendices are available to download from https://libraryjkp.papertrell.com/redeem using the code PAUNEZE

○ Chapter 1 ○

CREATIVITY

Psychologist Mihaly Csikszentmihályi (1996), one of the founders of positive psychology and a leading scholar on creativity, emphasized that the act of creating enables individuals to physically connect with their world around them, shape the symbolic domains in their culture in new ways, and create a tangible piece that mirrors their self-aspects. Dean Simonton (2000), another leading scholar on the concept of creativity, introduced a two-C model of creativity: Big-C creativity and little-c creativity. Big-C creativity is characterized by individuals' ability to create unique and innovative creations, while little-c creativity refers to individuals' ability to engage in daily acts of creations. A few years later, Kaufman and Beghetto (2009) extended Simonton's two-C model to a four-C model that includes as well a mini-c creativity (i.e., individuals engage in personal discoveries and devise creative solutions to achieve goals) and pro-c creativity (i.e., professional accomplishments).

In clinical settings, therapists, especially creative arts therapists, commonly design a nurturing environment wherein clients identify and engage in little-c and mini-c creativity. Hence, when administering arts activities to clients, there is greater emphasis on clients' creative processes (i.e., the effect the creative act has on clients) rather than on their creative products (i.e., clients' artistic accomplishment or the aesthetics of their final art-piece). Through the creative process, clients become curious, explore the environment with the senses, make autonomous decisions, and express their thoughts and feelings in a symbolic manner (Kramer, 1971; McNiff, 2009; Pennebaker & Smyth, 2016; Rubin, 1999). Further, modest acts of creativity have the potential to activate clients' imagination. According to Swiss psychologist Carl Jung, the act of imagination involves an individual in creating mental images of people, places, and objects that are not present to their senses in the here-and-now. Their mental images are based on their past memory, current life experiences, and future visions (Chodorow, 1997). Hence, the arts such as dance, drawings, and sculptures are the visible external products of individuals' internal mental images (Kast, 1992; Pelaprat & Cole, 2011). Regarding imagination, recently in the field of positive psychology, Martin Seligman and Scott Barry Kaufman launched the Imagination Institute in order to investigate the concept of imagination in greater depth (Kaufman, 2014).

The following arts activities are designed for clients to identify their personal creative outlets, reconnect with their little-c creativity, awaken their active imagination, engage in sensory play with their outer world, and maintain their color and pattern recognition skills.

The creative arts materials needed for the activities are outlined in Table 1.1.

Table 1.1 Creative arts materials

Paper	multi-sized drawing paper (8.5" x 11", 12" x 14", 14" x 17", 18" x 24"), colored construction paper, crepe paper, origami paper, poster paper, tissue paper, colored post-it square paper, scrapbook paper, journal paper, watercolor paper
Drawing materials	pencils, pen, gel pens, colored markers, colored pencils, oil pastels, soft pastels

Paint materials	acrylic paint, acrylic paint markers, acrylic paint sticks, watercolor
Collage materials	beads buttons, cardboard boxes, craft sticks, coffee stir sticks, cork, fabric, feathers, gems, ribbon, decorated rubber stamps, matte board, newspaper, magazine images, pipe cleaners, string, thread, tiles, shoe boxes, tin boxes
Nature materials	bark, beach glass, branches, drift wood, dry flowers, feathers, pebbles, pine cones, sand, shells, stones
Sculpting materials	soft clay, air-drying clay, foam blocks, lightweight wire, clay tools (i.e., wooden spoon and spatula), plaster sheets and mask mold for mask-making
General materials	glue, glitter glue, masking tape, scotch tape, painters tape, scissors, stapler, staples, multi-sized paint brushes, paint palettes, paper plates, stencils, poster board
Miniature symbols	characters (cartoon, fairy tale), wild animals (elephant, giraffe, horse, koala, monkey, rabbit, turtle), domestic animals (dog, cat), birds (dove, duck, penguin), trees, transportation vehicles (car, bus, plane, bicycle, truck), places (pyramids, Eiffel tower, Golden Gate Bridge), crystal, feather, door, watch, teapot, candle, decorated wooden egg, sea shell, beaded bracelet, whistle, keys, squishy balls, mini bells
Flow-inducing music	*Jeux D'eau*, by Cirque de Soleil *Jungle Book*, by Piano Guys *Story of My Life* (One Direction), by Piano Guys *Earth Song*, by Amadeus Electric Quartet *O*, by Cirque de Soleil
Relaxation music	Nature music Tibetan or Himalayan singing bowl sounds

1.1
SYMBOLIC CONNECTIONS

Materials

Neutral-positive oriented miniature symbols (see Table 1.1).

Procedure

1. Note that a symbol is a sign used to represent a mental image, object, meaning, or process.

2. Explore the miniature symbols dispersed on the table in front of you.

3. Select one symbol that intrigues you the most, or you feel attracted to, which evokes a positive memory or emotion.

4. Pick up the symbol and hold it in your hand. Discuss why you chose this particular object.

Discussion

• How is this symbol connected to a positive past memory, a current life experience, or a future vision?

• Which positive experience did the symbol elicit?

• Can you determine the emotions associated with the symbol?

• Allow the symbol to speak to you. What positive message is the object relaying, if any?

Note

This activity can be beneficial in the early stages of therapy, especially as a warm-up activity, to elicit a verbal dialogue between the client and the therapist.

1.2
IMAGINE THAT

Materials

Colored markers or pencils, *Imagine that activity sheet* (see Appendix A).

Procedure

1. Copy the *Imagine that activity sheet.*

2. Develop the three V shapes into a symbol or symbols (e.g., person, place, or object). You can create one symbol using all three Vs or three separate symbols with each V.

3. Provide a title for your image.

4. If time permits, create a story using the symbol(s).

Discussion

• What did you imagine?

• What symbol(s) arose?

• Is/are the symbol(s) related to a past memory, a current life experience, or a future vision?

1.3
IMAGINATIVE CHAIR MOVEMENT

Materials

Chairs (in a group setting, set up chairs in a round circle), *Walking through a Meadow* guided imagery script (see below).

Procedure

1. The therapist reads the following *Walking through a Meadow* guided imagery script out loud while the individual or group members imagine and engage in basic body movements:

    Walking through a Meadow
    While sitting, we are going on an imaginary walk with our imaginative basket. Pick up your basket and let us start by walking on a path. Lift your legs up and down. The path leads us to a meadow filled with a variety of wild flowers. We walk towards the center of the meadow and then stop for a brief moment. We reach down to pick up a flower. What flower do you see? With your right arm, pick and smell the flower, then place the flower in your basket. Now let us continue walking. Lift your legs up and down. At the other end of the meadow is an orchard with a line of fruit trees. Let us walk towards the orchard. With your left arm, reach and pick a fruit from one of the trees. What type of fruit did you pick? Place the fruit in your basket and let us continue walking in the meadow. Lift your legs up and down. The meadow leads us to another path. This path leads us to a pond. What type of fish do you see in the pond? Continue walking, lifting your legs up and down. We finally reach the original path that brings us back to the room.

Discussion

- What color was the flower, fruit, fish?

- What shape was your basket?

- Was the meadow a familiar place?

Note

This guided imagery activity is well suited to older adults with limited or restricted body movement.

1.4
SPONTANEOUS SCRIBBLE

Materials

Colored markers or pencils, large drawing paper (12" x 14" or 14" x 17"), tape.

Procedure

1. Select a single colored marker or pencil that is bold and you can see clearly.

2. Tape the large drawing paper on a table in front of you.

3. With your eyes open or closed, scribble around with your drawing instrument on the paper for approximately one minute.

4. When you complete your scribble, remove the tape and hold your scribble drawing at arm's length.

5. Look at your scribble drawing at different angles. Do you see a symbol or symbols in your scribble? Do you see a person, place, or thing?

6. Now with multiple colors, bring the symbol(s) into clear focus.

7. Provide a title for your image.

Discussion

• What symbol(s) emerged from your scribble drawing?

• Is/are the symbol(s) (i.e., person, place, or thing) connected to your past, present, or future life in any way?

Simple modification

Alternatively, the therapist can administer the *Spontaneous scribble activity sheet* for clients who find a blank sheet of paper overwhelming (see Appendix B).

Note

The spontaneous scribble drawing was developed by art educator Florence Cane (1951). The drawing activity can be used by the therapist to examine if a client has the imaginative thinking ability to draw and develop symbolic representations of people, places, or things not present to their senses from their abstract scribble lines (Darewych, Newton, & Farrugie, 2018). If clients do not imagine a symbol or symbols during the first administration, the drawing activity can be re-administered during a future session. The *Scribble drawing rating scale* (Darewych 2017a; see Appendix C) or the Hunter Imagination Questionnaire (Jung, Flores, & Hunter, 2016) can be used when administering the arts activity as an assessment tool in clinical or research settings.

Case example

Figure 1.1 depicts a spontaneous scribble created by Lisa (pseudonym), a young adult with high-functioning autism, during a single study session investigating imagination in adults with autism spectrum disorder (ASD) (Darewych *et al.*, 2018). Lisa developed her scribble lines with red dots into a "quilt" that represents a quilt she recently helped her mom make as a wedding gift. The arts activity enabled Lisa to reflect on a meaningful activity she recently created with a significant family member.

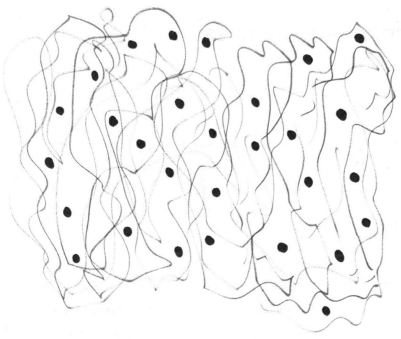

Figure 1.1 Scribble drawing

1.5
CREATIVE OUTLETS

Materials

Drawing paper, colored markers or pencils, oil pastels, pencil, eraser. Three-dimensional (3D) option: multi-colored quick air-drying clay.

Procedure

1. Reflect on your past and current life experiences. What creative outlets or activities did you participate in? Was it playing an instrument, baking, singing, or photography? What creative outlet(s) do you currently engage in that calms your state of mind?

2. Draw or sculpt your current creative outlet(s).

Discussion

- Do you connect with your current creative outlet(s) frequently?
- Which creative outlet(s) calm(s) you?
- What, or who, nurtures your creativity?
- What, or who, blocks your creativity?
- What new creative outlet(s) would you like to explore in the future?

Note

Creativity is also an important character strength under the virtue of wisdom and knowledge (see Chapter 4).

1.6
SENSORY SACK

Materials

A small sack filled with found sensory stimulating objects such as feathers, buttons, seashells, cork, crepe paper, foam blocks, squishy balls, and mini-bells (see Table 1.1).

Procedure

1. Place the small sack filled with sensory stimulating objects on your lap or on the table in front of you.

2. Insert your hand into the sack and explore the objects. Notice the different sensations.

3. When ready, remove the most sensory appealing object from the sack and spend a few minutes exploring the object that intrigues you the most.

Discussion

- Which sensory object intrigued you the most?

- While connecting with this object, did you experience any positive emotions, thoughts, or memories?

- Was there a sensory object you shifted your hand away from?

- What other objects, places, or events in your life stimulate your senses in a pleasant manner?

○ Chapter 2 ○

FLOW

Creativity often involves the process of flow. Csikszentmihályi (1991, 1996) conceptualized flow as a positive state of consciousness when individuals are fully engaged in an activity during which they lose track of time and disconnect from their physical surroundings and life stressors. Being in a state of flow is commonly referred to as "being in the zone," especially by athletes. During a flow-inducing activity, individuals may become immersed in a physical and mental state of transcendence and may not be consciously aware of any particular emotions. At the end of a flow-inducing activity, however, individuals may experience positive emotions such as awe, joy, and serenity (Csikzentmihályi, 1997).

Research has demonstrated that flow-inducing art-making experiences can reduce negative feelings such as fears and helplessness (Reynolds & Prior, 2006).

The following arts activities invite clients in therapeutic sessions to engage in flow-inducing creative acts, disconnect from life stressors, and calm their state of mind. When introducing these flow-inducing arts activities, it is important that the therapist set up a space in which the client can move freely and create with fluid art materials such as acrylic paints, watercolor paints, or soft clay. Additionally, sufficient time (one to three hours) is recommended for clients to immerse themselves in flow processes. Therapists can couple these arts activities with the Flow State Scale (Jackson & Marsh, 1996).

2.1
CALMING COLORS

Materials

Drawing paper, soft pastels or acrylic paint sticks, relaxation music (optional; see Table 1.1).

Procedure

1. Sit comfortably in a chair. Relax and take a few deep breaths.

2. When ready, color in the entire paper with colors that make you feel calm and relaxed. You can engage in this calming activity in silence or while listening to meditation or relaxation music. Allow the peaceful and soothing sounds to calm your mind.

3. When you complete your drawing, provide a title for your image.

Discussion

- Explore how these colors make you feel.

- What elements in your life are calming?

- How can you introduce these calming colors in your surroundings (i.e., home, school, work)?

- What other activities make you feel calm?

Supervision variation

Supervisors direct supervisees to reflect on how they can create a safe and comfortable therapy room for them and their clients to feel calm. For example, explore communication styles, colors, and relaxation objects that can be brought into the therapy room.

2.2
CELTIC ART MANDALYNTH

Materials

Trinity Celtic art mandalynth activity sheet (see Appendix D); a capped pen, coffee stir, or chopstick.

Procedure

1. Copy the Trinity Celtic art mandalynth.

2. Commence tracing the path knots anywhere with your chosen instrument. While tracing the path knots, cross over intersections. There are no decisions to make while tracing the path knots. Simply follow the free-flowing pathway of the design and end at any time or when you have reached a calm state of mind.

Discussion

- How did you feel after the activity?

- What other free-flowing and rhythmic activities can you engage in?

Note

Celtic art mandalynths were created by Celtic artist Erin Rado, who also goes by the art name Ravensdaughter (2016). Ravensdaughter's mandala designs are based on classic Celtic art that focuses on the overall pathway of the intertwining knot. Tracing a Celtic art mandalynth is more like doodling than coloring. There are three categories of Celtic art mandalynth designs: open, medium, and tight. Open mandalynth designs are soothing to trace, have a rhythmic count, and are best for relaxing an unsettled mind. Medium mandalynth designs also have a nice flow but are more challenging to trace and are best for individuals with a ruminating mind which struggles with concentrating. Tight mandalynth designs are less relaxing and difficult to trace. They are best for individuals who enjoy solving challenging puzzles.

2.3
ZESTY FLOW

Materials

Large drawing paper (14" x 17", 18" x 24"), acrylic paint markers or sticks, oil pastels, instrumental music with energetic rhythms (see Table 1.1).

Procedure

1. While standing or sitting, stretch your body. Shake your hands and allow your dominant hand to create figures of eight, six to eight times, in front of you.

2. Tape the large drawing paper on a table or on the wall.

3. Take a few breaths and begin playing the selected rhythmic music.

4. Select a single art instrument and commence drawing on paper or painting on canvas while listening to the energizing and uplifting music. Draw or paint and move until the music stops (five to eight minutes).

Discussion

• What other activities or music shift you into a state of flow?

• What elements (i.e., people, places, and things) energize you?

• What elements take you out of flow?

2.4
FLOW-FREE WRITING

Materials

Pen or pencil, paper or journal book.

Procedure

1. Write on a piece of paper, or in your journal book, all the spontaneous thoughts and emotions that are currently spiraling in your mind in an expressive and flowing way. While writing, there is no need to focus on grammar or punctuation.

2. When you have finished writing, read your flow-free writing and circle three to four words that intrigue you the most. Explore the meanings associated with the key words.

Discussion

- Which spontaneous thoughts and emotions presented themselves in your writing?

- Which key words did you circle?

- Are any of the words connected to a past memorable moment, current life experience, or a future aspiration?

○ Chapter 3 ○

POSITIVE EMOTIONS

For decades now, scholars and researchers have been studying human emotions. Both positive and negative emotions are essential for healthy functioning and human flourishing. Positive emotions such as love, joy, serenity, and awe provide individuals with pleasant responses to life situations and make them feel good. However, negative emotions such as anger, fear, guilt, and loneliness provide individuals with unpleasant responses to situations that have a tendency to drag them down. Yet negative emotions are critical for human survival, for they alert individuals to problematic circumstances and enable them to act quickly under dangerous situations (Turner, 2000).

In 1998, psychologist Barbara Fredrickson proposed the *broaden-and-build theory* to better understand positive emotions. The theory stresses that positive emotions broaden individuals' thinking processes and perceptions and build stable psychological and social resources (e.g., relationships, coping skills). Further, when appropriately induced, positive emotions have the ability to mitigate negative emotions (Fredrickson, 1998). Research has shown that individuals who experience more positive emotions exhibit greater happiness and well-being (Diener *et al.*, 1999), live longer (Diener & Chan, 2011), and establish healthy relationships (Fredrickson, 1998). Yet, due to the *negativity bias*—an evolutionary mechanism—individuals tend to focus on their negative emotions and life struggles rather than on their positive emotions and meaningful life moments (Vaish, Grossmann, & Woodward, 2008).

In one compelling study, Fredrickson and Losada (2005) presented the *positivity ratio*. The ratio consists of three positive emotions to one negative emotion (3:1). In order to function well and to flourish, individuals need to experience three times more positive emotions than negative emotions. Individuals at the beginning of their therapeutic journey tend to experience a lower ratio of positive emotions to negative emotions. Therefore, it is the task of the therapist to generate more positive emotions in their clients. Recent research findings have found that the act of making art can reduce negative emotions, while at the same time improving mood and increasing positive emotions, in individuals over a brief timeframe (Babouchkina & Robbins, 2015).

The following arts activities have the potential to elicit positive emotions such as joy and hope in clients. Additionally, these arts activities direct clients to identify negative and positive emotions, consider their passions, and engage in the act of gratitude.

3.1
POSITIVITY PALETTE

Materials

Colored markers or pencils, *Positivity palette activity sheet* (see Appendix E).

Procedure

1. Refer to Barbara Fredrickson's (2009) "positivity palette," which includes states of "joy, gratitude, serenity, interest, hope, pride, amusement, inspiration, awe, and love" (p.53).

2. Copy the *Positivity palette activity sheet*.

3. Color in the five palette shapes with colors that you believe are cheerful, calming, joyful, and hopeful.

Discussion

• Are you surrounded by these colors in your current life in any way?

• What colors do you wear to uplift your spirits?

• How can you bring these colors to your life?

• What colors drag you down?

• What, or who, brings positive emotions such as joy to your life?

• What is happening in your life that is good?

- What, or who, makes you laugh?

- Which positive emotions did you savor today or this week?

Note

When working with younger clients, therapists can read the children's book *I Feel Teal*, written by Lauren Rille and illustrated by Aimée Sicuro. The book describes a person's personal color palette of feelings.

3.2
POETIC POSITIVES

Materials

Pen or pencil and writing paper.

Procedure

1. Write down all the words that you can think of that make you feel good and uplift your spirits. If time permits, put as many of these words together to make a short poem.

Discussion

*   What positive words and phrases can counter the negative thoughts that fill your mind?

*   Can you put the words together to make a short poem?

3.3
FAVORITE KIND OF DAY

Materials

Drawing paper, colored markers or pencils.

Procedure

1. Using colors, shapes, and symbols, draw your favorite kind of day.

Discussion

- What does your favorite day look like?

- What activities do you engage in during your favorite day?

- What favorite activities elicit positive emotions in you?

- What is your favorite environment?

Note

The favorite kind of day drawing activity was developed by Manning (1987). Another similar activity is Seligman's (2011) "A beautiful day" which directs a client to design a beautiful day. The client could draw symbols that represent the elements (i.e., people, places, and things) that make it a beautiful day.

Case example

Figure 3.1 portrays a favorite kind of day drawing created by Katie (pseudonym), a young adult with high-functioning autism, during a group digital art therapy session. Katie created her drawing on a digital canvas, using the Fresh Paint application on a password-protected Windows 10 touchscreen laptop. With her eyes open, Katie drew a brown pizza with her favorite toppings of cheese, pepperoni, and green peppers. On reflection, Katie stated, "My favorite kind of day is making my favorite pizza with my mom." The image opened a dialogue between Katie and other group members around other favorite daily and weekend pursuits with friends and family members.

Figure 3.1 Favorite kind of day

3.4
HOPE RITUAL

Materials

Mason glass jar with lid or shoebox, scrap-book or origami paper, magazine quotes and images, colored markers, items to embellish the jar or shoebox.

Procedure

1. Note that hopeful feelings and thoughts help individuals strive for a better life and establish pathways towards future goals.

2. Write your hope(s) on small sheets of paper. Fold the sheets and add them to your hope jar or box. You can also add images of the elements (i.e., people, places, and things) or hopeful quotes that make you feel more hopeful.

Discussion

*   What does hope mean to you?

*   What, or who, gives you hope?

*   Recall a time when you felt hopeless. What, or who, made you feel hopeful again?

*   What other hope-filled rituals can you engage in?

Note

Hope is also an important character strength under the virtue of transcendence (see Chapter 4).

3.5
GRATITUDE CARD

Materials

Colored markers or pencils, origami paper, card paper and envelopes.

Procedure

1. Note that gratitude is being thankful for the good things that have happened to you and taking time to express thanks to others (Peterson & Seligman, 2004).

2. Think about one person who has recently made a positive impact on your life emotionally, physically, or spiritually.

3. With the materials provided, create a gratitude card for this person whom you would like to express your thanks to.

4. Mail or personally deliver the card to the special person.

Discussion

• How has this person helped you become a better person?

• What act of kindness did this person carry out for you?

• What are you grateful for today?

• What act of kindness can you perform today?

Note

Gratitude is also an important character strength under the virtue of transcendence (see Chapter 4).

3.6
GRATITUDE SCROLL

Materials

Small canvas, white acrylic paint, pre-cut magazine images, quotes, found objects, rubber stamps. For drawing adaptation, use the *Gratitude scroll activity sheet* (see Appendix F).

Procedure

1. Note that gratitude is being thankful for the good things that have happened to you and taking time to express thanks to others (Peterson & Seligman, 2004).

2. With the materials provided, create a gratitude scroll for a person who you appreciate having in your current life or who has impacted your life in a positive way. Layer the scroll with found objects and messages of thankfulness.

3. Deliver the rolled-up scroll to the significant person.

Discussion

- How has this person helped you become a better person?

- What act of kindness has this person carried out for you?

- What are you grateful for today?

Note

The gratitude scroll mixed-media activity was designed by art therapist Cathy Malchiodi (2002) and can be coupled with the six-item Gratitude Questionnaire (McCullough, Emmons, & Tsang, 2002).

Supervision variation

Supervisors can request supervisees to explore self-gratitude—being grateful for oneself.

Case example

Figure 3.2 depicts a self-gratitude scroll created by psychotherapist Cynthia (pseudonym) during a supervision session as an opportunity to explore her relationship to her inner spirit. Cynthia created her self-gratitude scroll using beads, canvas, paint, fabric, magazine images, ribbon, and wire. The following is Cynthia's free-writing associated with her gratitude scroll: "The inner flame that helps me hold strength and focus as I work. It reminds me of the gratitude I have towards nature and the interconnection of all things as a resource."

Figure 3.2 Gratitude Scroll

3.7
VIRTUAL GRATITUDE VISIT

Materials

Two chairs.

Procedure

1. Note that gratitude is being thankful for the good things that have happened to you and taking time to express thanks to others (Peterson & Seligman, 2004).

2. Sit comfortably in one of the chairs for this activity. Face the empty chair across from you. Imagine that the person to whom you would like to express your gratitude is sitting in the empty chair across from you.

3. Commence the role play by verbally thanking the person for all the things that they have done for you. You may thank them for the acts of kindness, their emotional support for you during challenging life moments.

4. When you have completed expressing your gratitude to them, reverse roles. Shift to the other chair and become the other person receiving the gratitude. Give voice to the other person. Allow the other person to voice their thoughts and feelings around the gratitude which they have just received.

5. Now shift back to your original chair and become yourself again.

Discussion

- What was it like to express your gratitude to the other person?

- What was it like to take on the role of the other person receiving the gratitude?

- What other emotions did this dramatic role-play activity elicit in you?

Note

The virtual gratitude visit was developed by psychologist and psychodrama therapist Dan Tomasulo (2019) for clients who are unable to partake in a gratitude visit due to the person not being available (e.g., the person has passed away), but are still interested in expressing their appreciation for that person who is not around.

3.8
HARMONIOUS AND OBSESSIVE PASSION

Materials

Colored markers, pencils, or pastels, and *Circle activity sheet* (see Appendix G).

Procedure

1. Refer to psychologist Robert Vallerand's (2013) book entitled *The Psychology of Passion*, describes passion as a process of engaging in a cherished activity that an individual believes is part of their personal identity. Vallerand further explains that there are two types of passion: harmonious and obsessive. Harmonious passion refers to an individual's tendency to regularly engage in an activity that they adore, find meaningful, and have control over, whereas obsessive passion refers to an individual's inclination to partake in an activity that they find less pleasurable and meaningful, and have less control over. Harmonious passion often leads to healthy behaviors, while obsessive passion can lead to less healthy behaviors.

2. Copy the *Circle activity sheet*.

3. Divide the circle into two sections in any way.

4. In one section, draw an activity that you are passionate about, find enjoyable and meaningful, have control over, and that brings harmony to your life.

5. In the other section, draw an activity that you are passionate about yet heavily fixate on, which leads you to engage in less healthy behaviors.

6. When finished, provide a title for your drawing.

7. Discuss your harmonious and obsessive passions.

Discussion

- What activity are you passionate about that brings harmony and joy to your life?

- What activity are you passionate about but obsess over?

- What, or who, sparks your passion?

- How can you curtail your obsessive passion?

- How can you transform your obsessive passion into a harmonious passion?

Simple modification

To simplify this arts activity, the therapist can invite the client to reflect on and then draw in the circle one activity they are passionate about.

○ Chapter 4 ○

CHARACTER STRENGTHS

Character strengths are positive traits reflected in one's thoughts, feelings, and behaviors which help one to overcome life stressors (Park, Peterson, & Seligman, 2004). In 2004, psychologists Christopher Peterson and Martin Seligman developed a manual introducing the Values in Action (VIA) Classification of 24 Character Strengths and Virtues. The classification system delineates six human virtues (i.e., wisdom and knowledge, courage, humanity, justice, temperance, and transcendence) that are subdivided into 24 character strengths (e.g., bravery, creativity, curiosity, kindness, and teamwork). In clinical and research settings, the list of 24 character strengths enables individuals to identify, define, and describe their greatest positive traits. Table 4.1 displays the VIA Classification—six core virtues with their corresponding character strengths. Character strengths are universal, interdependent of one another (e.g., kindness and humility), expressed in varying degrees under certain situations (e.g., social, work, family), and may change during the individual's developmental lifespan in response to life experiences (Niemiec, 2013, 2014, 2018). Peterson and Seligman specified that individuals typically possess three to seven top character strengths—so-called "signature" strengths.

When individuals own and appreciate their signature strengths, they feel more genuine and inspired to apply them in their daily lives (Peterson & Seligman, 2004).

A few years later, the VIA Inventory of Strengths (VIA-IS), also referred to as the VIA Survey, was developed to measure individuals' character strengths (Park & Peterson, 2006). The valid and reliable VIA-IS is currently a free, online self-report questionnaire that ranks individuals' character strengths from highest to lowest. Recent empirical research in positive psychology examining the concept of character strengths has linked the use of character strengths with greater levels of life satisfaction (Park *et al.*, 2004), post-traumatic growth (Peterson *et al.*, 2008), and well-being (Seligman *et al.*, 2005).

According to psychologist Niemiec (2014), character strengths work in clinical practice is a three-step process that includes the following: awareness, exploration, and application. A client must first understand the language of strengths and become aware of their character strengths. Once they gain awareness of their character strengths, they can explore their strengths in greater depth through reflective journaling. Following the self-reflective process, the client cultivates a number of strengths in their daily life and uses their strengths in new ways, often as action-oriented homework assignments.

The following arts activities enable clients to identify, build on, and honor their character strengths in creative ways. In clinical settings, especially in brief cognitive behavioral or solution-focused sessions, the therapist can direct these arts activities as homework assignments and invite clients to complete the online VIA Survey to obtain a better understanding of their strongest and weakest character strengths.

Table 4.1 VIA Classification of 24 Character Strengths and Virtues

1. **Wisdom and knowledge:** Cognitive strengths that entail the acquisition and use of knowledge.
• *Creativity* [originality, ingenuity]: Thinking of novel and productive ways to conceptualize and do things; includes artistic achievement but is not limited to it.
• *Curiosity* [interest, novelty-seeking, openness to experience]: Taking an interest in ongoing experience for its own sake; finding subjects and topics fascinating; exploring and discovering.
• *Judgment* [critical thinking]: Thinking things through and examining them from all sides; not jumping to conclusions; being able to change one's mind in light of evidence; weighing all evidence fairly.
• *Love of learning:* Mastering new skills, topics, and bodies of knowledge, whether on one's own or formally; obviously related to the strength of curiosity but goes beyond it to describe the tendency to add systematically to what one knows.
• *Perspective* [wisdom]: Being able to provide wise counsel to others; having ways of looking at the world that make sense to oneself and to other people.
2. **Courage:** Emotional strengths that involve the exercise of will to accomplish goals in the face of opposition, external or internal.
• *Bravery* [valor]: Not shrinking from threat, challenge, difficulty, or pain; speaking up for what is right even if there is opposition; acting on convictions even if unpopular; includes physical bravery but is not limited to it.
• *Perseverance* [persistence, industriousness]: Finishing what one starts; persisting in a course of action in spite of obstacles; "getting it out the door"; taking pleasure in completing tasks.
• *Honesty* [authenticity, integrity]: Speaking the truth but more broadly presenting oneself in a genuine way and acting in a sincere way; being without pretense; taking responsibility for one's feelings and actions.
• *Zest* [vitality, enthusiasm, vigor, energy]: Approaching life with excitement and energy; not doing things halfway or half-heartedly; living life as an adventure; feeling alive and activated.

3. **Humanity:** Interpersonal strengths that involve tending and befriending others.

- *Love:* Valuing close relations with others, in particular those in which sharing and caring are reciprocated; being close to people.
- *Kindness* [generosity, nurturance, care, compassion, altruistic love, "niceness"]: Doing favors and good deeds for others; helping them; taking care of them.
- *Social intelligence* [emotional intelligence, personal intelligence]: Being aware of the motives and feelings of other people and oneself; knowing what to do to fit into different social situations; knowing what makes other people tick.

4. **Justice:** Civic strengths that underlie healthy community life.

- *Teamwork* [citizenship, social responsibility, loyalty]: Working well as a member of a group or team; being loyal to the group; doing one's share.
- *Fairness:* Treating all people the same according to notions of fairness and justice; not letting personal feelings bias decisions about others; giving everyone a fair chance.
- *Leadership:* Encouraging a group of which one is a member to get things done and at the time maintaining good relations within the group; organizing group activities and seeing that they happen.

5. **Temperance:** Strengths that protect against excess.

- *Forgiveness:* Forgiving those who have done wrong; accepting the shortcomings of others; giving people a second chance; not being vengeful.
- *Humility:* Letting one's accomplishments speak for themselves; not regarding oneself as more special than one is.
- *Prudence:* Being careful about one's choices; not taking undue risks; not saying or doing things that might later be regretted.
- *Self-regulation* [self-control]: Regulating what one feels and does; being disciplined; controlling one's appetites and emotions.

6. **Transcendence:** Strengths that forge connections to the larger universe and provide meaning.

- *Appreciation of beauty and excellence* [awe, wonder, elevation]: Noticing and appreciating beauty, excellence, and/or skilled performance in various domains of life, from nature to art to mathematics to science to everyday experience.

- *Gratitude:* Being aware of and thankful for the good things that happen; taking time to express thanks.

- *Hope* [optimism, future-mindedness, future orientation]: Expecting the best in the future and working to achieve it; believing that a good future is something that can be brought about.

- *Humor* [playfulness]: Liking to laugh and tease; bringing smiles to other people; seeing the light side; making (not necessarily telling) jokes.

- *Spirituality* [faith, purpose]: Having coherent beliefs about the higher purpose and meaning of the universe; knowing where one fits within the larger scheme; having beliefs about the meaning of life that shape conduct and provide comfort.

4.1
STRENGTHS STONES

Materials

Flat stones collected from the beach, list of VIA 24 character strengths (see Table 4.1), acrylic paint or paint markers.

Procedure

1. Read and familiarize yourself with the VIA 24 character strengths (Peterson & Seligman, 2004).

2. From the list, identify one character strength that you believe you hold.

3. Select one stone.

4. On one side of the stone, write down your character strength.

5. On the other side of the stone, depict a symbol representing your character strength.

6. Add colors to both sides of the stone.

Discussion

• What character strength did you depict on the stone?

• How did you use this character strength in the past to overcome a life challenge?

• What resources help you fortify this character strength?

- Did you use this character strength today in any way?

- How can you celebrate this character strength?

Supervision variation

Supervisors ask supervisees to identify a strength they could use in a future session with a challenging client.

Note

This simple character strengths arts activity is suitable for clients who are unaware of their strengths and have a difficult time discussing them. One homework assignment would be to invite clients to ask a family member or a close friend to identify one unique strength that they hold.

4.2
STRENGTHS COLLAGE

Materials

Poster board, magazine images, scissors, glue, tape, markers, glitter, gems, rubber stamps, list of VIA 24 character strengths (see Table 4.1).

Procedure

1. Read and familiarize yourself with the VIA 24 character strengths (Peterson & Seligman, 2004).

2. From the list, identify what you believe to be your top five character strengths, also known as signature strengths.

3. With the materials provided, create a collage on poster board with the magazine images that symbolically illustrate what you believe to be your top five character strengths.

4. Embellish your strengths collage in any way using the art materials provided.

5. Discuss your top five character strengths.

Discussion

•   What do you believe are your top five character strengths?

•   How do you apply your five character strengths at home, school, or work?

- Which two or three character strengths can you use to overcome a present problem in your life?

- Which character strengths emerged from your cultural background or experiences?

- What is your weakest strength?

- Which character strengths do you want to make stronger?

- Which character strengths are you most proud of?

- How can you celebrate your character strengths?

- In a group setting, voice the strengths you appreciate about your family members, classmates, or co-workers.

Supervision variation

Supervisors prompt supervisees to identify their top five character strengths and describe how they apply these character strengths when working with clients. Allow supervisees to discuss how these character strengths enable them to support their clients. Supervisees can also take a moment to identify their clients' character strengths.

Note

For further reading on the strengths collage, see Darewych and Riedel Bowers (2017).

Case example

Figure 4.1 portrays a strengths collage created by Gregory (pseudonym), a youth orphan who attended a strengths-based psycho-education workshop in Ukraine. During the workshop, Gregory and other group members were introduced to the universal VIA 24 character strengths (Peterson & Seligman, 2004) in English and Ukrainian and prompted to create a strengths collage with pre-selected magazine images and colored markers symbolizing at least five of their character strengths. Gregory created his collage on a bright yellow poster board which included images and words that embodied his character strengths of "curiosity, fairness, kindness, love, spirituality." The strengths collage arts activity provided Gregory with the opportunity to establish a vocabulary of strengths, creatively reflect on his strengths, voice his strengths in the group setting, and become aware of strengths in others.

Figure 4.1 Strengths collage

4.3
STRENGTHS SHIELD

Materials

Cardboard, fabric, felt pieces, wood, acrylic paint markers or sticks, glue, scissors, list of VIA 24 character strengths (see Table 4.1).

Procedure

1. Read and familiarize yourself with the VIA 24 character strengths (Peterson & Seligman, 2004).

2. From the list, identify what you believe to be your top five character strengths, also known as signature strengths.

3. With the materials provided, create a strengths shield that symbolically illustrates what you believe to be your top five character strengths.

4. Embellish your strengths shield in any way using the materials provided.

5. Discuss your top five character strengths.

Discussion

- What do you believe are your top five character strengths?

- How do you apply these character strengths at home, school, or work?

- Which two or three character strengths can you use to overcome a present problem in your life?

- Which character strengths emerged from your cultural background or experiences?

- What is your weakest character strength?

- Which character strengths do you want to make stronger?

- Which character strengths are you most proud of?

- How can you celebrate your character strengths?

- In a group setting, voice the character strengths you appreciate about your family members, classmates, or co-workers.

4.4
STRENGTHS ATOM

Materials

Multi-sized styrofoam balls or plasticine, toothpicks, colored markers, list of VIA 24 character strengths (see Table 4.1).

Procedure

1. Read and familiarize yourself with the VIA 24 character strengths (Peterson & Seligman, 2004).

2. From the list, identify what you believe to be your top five character strengths, also referred to as your signature strengths.

3. Create a 3D strengths atom sculpture depicting your top five character strengths. Commence by writing your name or "I" on one of the atoms. Now select five other atom balls in varying sizes that will symbolically represent your top five character strengths. Write the name or letter of each character strength (e.g., C for Curiosity, L for Love of learning) on each atom ball. Allow the largest atom ball to represent the strongest of your top five character strengths and the smallest atom to represent the weakest. Now begin connecting the five atoms to your central "I" atom with the toothpicks that vary in length. When you have finished making your 3D strengths atom sculpture, discuss the placement and the dynamics of each strengths atom. If time permits, give voice to each strengths atom by starting with an "I am" sentence. For example, "I am Curiosity. I am closest to the strengths atom of Love of learning."

Discussion

- What do you believe are your top five character strengths?

- Which character strength atom is the strongest, largest, or most dominant?

- Which two character strength atoms are the closest?

- Which character strength atom was placed furthest away from the centered "I" atom?

- How do you apply your top five character strengths at home, school, or work?

- Which two or three character strengths can you use to overcome a present problem in your life?

- In a group setting, voice the character strengths you appreciate about your family members, classmates, or co-workers.

Drama variation in a group setting

The strengths atom can also be used in group role play (Tomasulo, 2018). In a group setting, clients can role-play the strengths atom. Each client has a chance to stand in the middle of the room while other group members stand and face the client at different distances related to the client. Each group member represents a strengths atom and offers a statement. Once all group members are in position, the client begins by walking towards the closest strength atom (e.g., Curiosity) and they reverse roles, each standing in the other's position. Once in the role of Curiosity, the client offers an "I am" statement. For example, "I am your Curiosity. I am closest to you because I entice you to always shift your perspective and work outside the box." The client then returns to their central position while the group member playing the Curiosity atom returns to their position and verbally delivers the statement back to the client.

Note

The strengths atom sculpture was adapted from Dan Tomasulo's (2018) strengths atom drawing activity.

4.5
TREE OF LIFE

Materials

Poster board or canvas, colored markers, colored pencils, oil pastels, soft pastels, acrylic paint markers or sticks, fabric, magazine images, list of VIA 24 character strengths (see Table 4.1). 3D option: soft clay, nature objects such as twigs, yarn, ribbon.

Procedure

1. Read and familiarize yourself with the VIA 24 character strengths (Peterson & Seligman, 2004).

2. From the list, identify what you believe are your top five character strengths which are also referred to as your signature strengths.

3. Draw or sculpt your life as a tree showing roots, trunk, branches, and leaves: the Tree of Life.

4. Allow the roots to represent your family, cultural, or ethnic roots.

5. Allow the trunk to represent your top five character strengths, skills, and talents.

6. Allow the branches to symbolize your hopes.

7. Allow the leaves to indicate the significant people in your life.

8. Include fruits that embody gifts such as acts of kindness.

Discussion

- What family traditions or rituals do you still cherish and take part in?

- What do you believe are your top five character strengths?

- What special skills and talents do you hold?

- What values are important to you?

- What are your hopes or aspirations?

- Who are the significant people in your life?

- What gifts do you give to people?

- Metaphorically, reflect on past storms that uprooted you and reflect on how you responded to challenging situations and which character strengths you used to protect yourself from such stormy weather.

Simple modification

Alternatively, the therapist can administer the *Tree of Life activity sheet* for clients who find a blank sheet of paper overwhelming (see Appendix H).

Supervision variation

Supervisors can invite supervisees to draw or sculpt a tree showing roots, trunk, branches, and leaves—a Tree of Life—and reflect on the following questions: What are the character strengths and values that you bring to your therapeutic sessions with clients? Which character strengths are embodied by the roots? What are your hopes and wishes for supervision? Who, or what, supports your clinical internship journey?

Note

This arts activity was adapted from Denborough's (2008) Tree of Life activity which was originally developed for children affected by HIV/AIDS in Africa.

4.6
STRENGTHS SPOTTER

Materials

Construction paper, origami paper, tissue paper, cardboard, fabric pieces, colored markers or paint markers, list of VIA 24 character strengths (see Table 4.1).

Procedure

1. Read and familiarize yourself with the VIA 24 character strengths (Peterson & Seligman, 2004).

2. A strengths spotter is a person who is aware of their character strengths as well as other people's (i.e., colleague's, partner's, friend's) strengths, values, and talents (Linley, 2008).

3. From the list, identify what you believe to be your top five character strengths which are also referred to as your signature strengths.

4. With the materials provided, create a strengths spotter hat.

5. On the inside of the hat, write or add symbols depicting your top five character strengths.

6. On the outside of the hat, write or depict symbols of the other person's character strengths.

Discussion

• What do you believe are your top five character strengths?

- What do you believe are the other person's top five character strengths?

- How can you celebrate your strengths?

- How can you celebrate the other person's strengths?

4.7
STRENGTHS STORIES

Materials

Children's books from around the world illustrating and describing human character strengths (see Table 4.2).

Procedure

1. Select a book from Table 4.2 illustrating and describing a character strength that you would like to learn more about.

Discussion

- What is the main character's strength(s)?

- How did the main character use their strength(s)?

- Did the main character use their strength(s) to overcome an obstacle?

- Did you use this strength in any way today or this week?

Note

In clinical settings, the strengths-based illustrated children's books can be placed in a basket in the waiting room. Each book can be used to ease transition from the waiting room to the therapy room. Once the young client settles in the therapy room with their book in hand, the therapist can invite the client to read the book to them. Alternatively, the therapist can finish reading the book to the client where they left off. The books presented in Table 4.2 are also great for adults who are open to reconnecting with their inner child.

Table 4.2 Strengths-based illustrated children's books

1. Creativity: *Beautiful Oops!* by Barney Saltzberg
2. Curiosity: *On a Beam of Light* by Jennifer Berne, illustrated by Vladimir Radunsky
3. Judgment: *Big Al* by Andrew Clements, illustrated by Yoshi Kogo
4. Love of learning: *Sergio Makes a Splash* by Edel Rodriguez
5. Perspective: *Through Your Eyes: My Child's Gift to Me* by Ainsley Earhardt, illustrated by Ji-Hyuk Kim
6. Bravery: *Brave Irene*, written and illustrated by William Steig
7. Perseverance: *The Little Engine That Could* by Waltz Piper, illustrated by George and Doris Hauman
8. Honesty: *Let's Be Honest*, written and illustrated by P. K. Hallinan
9. Zest: *Unstoppable Me* by Susan Verde, illustrated by Andrew Joyner
10. Love: *Love You Forever* by Robert Munsch, illustrated by Sheila McGraw
11. Kindness: *Have You Filled a Bucket Today?* by Carol McCloud, illustrated by David Messing
12. Social intelligence: *All About Feelings* by Felicity Brooks and Frankie Allen, illustrated by Mar Ferrero
13. Teamwork: *The Enormous Turnip* by Katie Daynes, illustrated by Geogien Overwater
14. Fairness: *That's Not Fair* by Gina and Mercer Mayer
15. Leadership: *Strega Nona* by Tomie dePaola
16. Forgiveness: *The Bear, the Piano, the Dog and the Fiddle* by David Litchfield

17. Humility: *The Tower* by Richard Paul Evans, illustrated by Jonathan Linton

18. Prudence: *Right and Wrong and Being Strong* by Lisa Engelhardt, illustrated by R. W. Alley

19. Self-regulation: *Grumpy Bird*, written and illustrated by Jeremy Tankard

20. Appreciation of beauty and excellence: *Stand Beautiful* by Chloe Howard, illustrated by Deborah Melmon

21. Gratitude: *Sylvester and the Magic Pebble*, written and illustrated by William Steig

22. Hope: *Cheerful Chick* by Martha Brockenbrough, illustrated by Brian Won

23. Humor: *Goodnight Gorilla*, written and illustrated by Peggy Rathmann

24. Spirituality: *Grandmother's Visit* by Betty Quan, illustrated by Carmen Mok

4.8
STRENGTHS AT THE MOVIES

Materials

Digital age stories, also known as movies (see Figure 4.2).

Procedure

1. Choose a character strength that you would like to explore in greater depth and then view the movie (the entire movie or a short clip from the movie) linked to that character strength (see Figure 4.2).

Discussion

- Which character strength did you decide to focus on?

- Which movie did you view?

- How did the main character use this strength?

- Did the main character use this strength to overcome an obstacle?

- How are you using this strength in your current life?

Note

Figure 4.2 depicts movies that are classified according to Peterson and Seligman's (2004) VIA 24 character strengths. The figure is taken from the book *Positive Psychology at the Movies: Using Films to Build Virtues and Character Strengths* (Niemiec & Wedding, 2008).

Short clips from these movies can illustrate various psychological principles and points. In clinical settings, clients can be encouraged to view the films as homework assignments and then used to expand the discussion of character strengths during future therapy sessions.

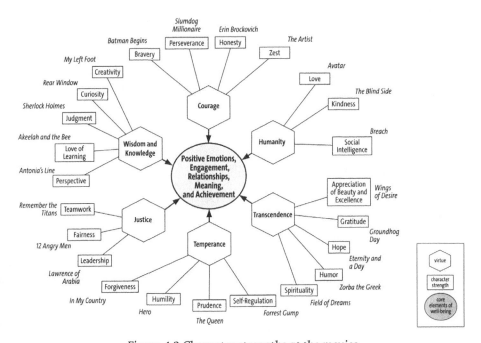

Figure 4.2 Character strengths at the movies

Adapted from Peterson & Seligman, 2004. The VIA Classification of Character Strengths and Virtues is copyright of the VIA Institute on Character. All rights reserved. Used with permission.

○ Chapter 5 ○

SELF-AWARENESS

Self-awareness is when individuals become consciously aware of their character strengths, weaknesses, positive and negative emotions, goals, needs, and cultural values. The benefit of self-awareness is that the conscious action enables individuals to regulate, improve, and adapt their behaviors (Baumeister & Vohs, 2004).

Post-modern theories of multiple selves (Lester, 2015; Markus & Nurius, 1986), roles (Landy, 1993), and self-aspects (McConnell, 2011) refute the notion that an individual has a single unified self. These theories emphasize that individuals are made of multiple self-aspects which develop out of their life experiences and collectively form who they are. Individuals who accept themselves for who they are and acknowledge their multiple aspects of self, including strong and weak attributes, generally possess a more positive attitude toward the self (Ryff & Keyes, 1995).

In clinical settings, the creative process encourages clients to undergo self-discovery (Kramer, 1971; Rubin, 1999). The following arts activities help clients gain greater awareness of their personal aspirations, self-aspects (past, present, and future), cultural identity, and values (see Table 5.1). Further, these arts activities continue to direct clients to reflect on their creativity, character strengths, and positive and negative emotions.

5.1
NESTING DOLL

Materials

One colorful stacked wooden nesting doll, colored pencils or markers, decorative scrap-book paper, scissors, glue, and multi-sized *Nesting doll activity sheet* (see Appendix I).

Procedure

1. The therapist presents a nesting doll and describes the self-aspect theory to clients: "Nesting dolls, also known as Matryoshka dolls, are colorful decorated wooden stacking dolls. The first nesting dolls were crafted in Russia and the name itself signifies motherhood. Today, masculine nesting dolls also exist. The doll's one-inside-another concept symbolically represents an individual's repertoire of self-aspects which are interconnected and continuously transforming in size and shape. Our self-aspects develop out of our life and cultural experiences and collectively form who we are. There are moments when our self-aspects harmoniously dance together in a circle. And then there are moments when certain self-aspects are engaged in a dragon fight."

2. Copy the *Nesting doll activity sheet*.

3. On reflection on the nesting doll, define five of your self-aspects with "I am" statements (e.g., I am a student, a friend, a parent, a volunteer).

4. With the materials provided, create your personal five-sized nesting doll ranking your five self-aspects from the most (largest) to the least

(smallest) prominent. The most prominent doll may represent your self-aspect that you typically project outward to the world, whereas your least prominent doll may characterize your core or vulnerable self-aspect.

5. When finished, look at each self-aspect individually and reflect on each self-aspect's character strengths (see Table 4.1) and values (see Table 5.1).

Discussion

• Which five self-aspects does your nesting doll depict?

• Which self-aspect is the largest (most prominent) in your current life?

• Which self-aspect is the smallest (least prominent) in your current life?

• What strengths and values does each self-aspect hold?

• Which self-aspect is currently undergoing growth or transformation?

• Which self-aspect(s) do your family members or colleagues primarily see?

Drama variation

Therapists can encourage clients to enact one of their self-aspects through drama by speaking out their inner strengths, values, aspirations, and unique qualities.

Supervisory variation

Supervisors could invite supervisees to reflect on how each distinct self-aspect may enhance and compromise the therapeutic alliance with current or future clients, and in what ways they are capable of supporting clients and themselves. The supervisor can direct the following:

- Describe your student, therapist intern, or therapist self-aspect.

- Which self-aspect is an active listener?

- Which self-aspect is a keen observer?

Note

For further reading on the nesting doll arts activity, see Riedel Bowers and Darewych (2019) and Darewych (2019).

Case example

Figure 5.1 depicts a five-size nesting doll created by Nicholas (pseudonym), who attended an intensive four-day group psycho-education workshop for youth orphans (aged 17–22) in Ukraine. During the second day of the workshop, the nesting doll arts activity was administered to all group members. Nicholas created his five-size nesting doll using the template and mandala patterned scrap-book paper. His nesting doll presents his self-aspects of (from most prominent to least prominent): "leader, scholarship recipient, designer, partner, and graduate student." After identifying each self-aspect, he wrote down on the back of his nesting doll two strengths and one value for each self-aspect. During the post-intervention group dialogue, Nicholas verbally described his "partner" self-aspect's character strength of love and his promising "designer" self-aspect's character strength of creativity. The nesting doll arts activity offered Nicholas and the other youth orphans in a group setting the opportunity to create a concrete art-piece of their inside and outside self-aspects. Moreover, the creative method encouraged them to envision their future professional self-aspects, and explore resources (i.e., people, places, and things) that will support their future professional self-aspects.

Figure 5.1 Nesting doll

Table 5.1 List of values

Achievement	Harmony	Reliability
Belonging	Honesty	Respect
Career	Inclusion	Security
Community	Independence	Solitude
Compassion	Joy	Structure
Cooperation	Justice	Success
Diversity	Leadership	Teamwork
Equality	Love	Thankfulness

Faith	Loyalty	Tranquility
Family	Openness	Vitality
Freedom	Order	Wisdom
Friendship	Peace	Wonder
Growth	Privacy	

5.2
BEST POSSIBLE SELF

Materials

One colorful stacked wooden nesting doll, colored pencils or markers, decorative paper, scissors, glue, and the *Nesting doll activity sheet* (see Appendix I).

Procedure

1. Copy the *Nesting doll activity sheet* and cut out the largest doll figure.

2. Take a moment to imagine yourself in the future, at your best and one year from now when you have achieved the goals you wanted to in life. With the art materials and the largest nesting doll figure, create your best possible self one year from now.

Discussion

- What will you be doing?

- Where will you be living?

- How will you be feeling?

- What will your top five character strengths be?

- Which life goals will you have achieved?

- Who will be part of your social circle?

- Is your best possible self realistic?

- What effects did this future-oriented activity have on you?

- Did the future-oriented activity motivate or inspire you in any way?

- Did the activity prompt you to make any changes in your current life in order to achieve your best possible self?

Note

This acts activity is adapted from Owens and Patterson's (2013) best possible selves drawing activity.

5.3
CULTURAL IDENTITY

Materials

Poster board, multi-colored paper, colored markers or pencils, glue, tape, scissors, magazine images. 3D option: plaster mask and acrylic paint.

Procedure

1. Refer to Corey and his colleagues (2015), who emphasized that one's culture is related to ethnicity, gender, race, religious background, socio-economic status, nationality, physical abilities or challenges, and sexual orientation.

2. Using the colors, shapes, symbols, words, and images, create a mask that symbolizes your cultural identity and values.

3. In a group setting, share your cultural identity mask with other members of the group. Which values are most important to you?

Discussion

- What does culture mean to you?

- What are some of your strongest values associated with your cultural background?

- What values do you want to let go of?

- What values do you want to keep?

- What cultural rituals, traditions, and celebrations do you still embrace?

Supervision variation

Supervisors can prompt supervisees to create their cultural identity mask and reflect on the following:

- How will your values affect your counseling work with clients?

- Reflect on the clients with whom you struggle to work with due to value differences or countertransference (e.g., clients who trigger personal needs, unresolved conflicts, or unfinished business).

- How can you become a culturally sensitive therapist?

Note

For further reading on the cultural identity arts activity, see Darewych (2019).

5.4
SUSTAINABLE SELF

Materials

Drawing paper, colored markers or pencils.

Procedure

1. There are moments in our lives when we feel burnt out, exhausted, overwhelmed, or stressed. Take a moment to reflect on the activities, hobbies, or interests that have helped you in the past and in your current life to disconnect from stressors and sustain your mental health and wellness.

2. Now draw a picture of one of your self-care activities.

3. When finished, provide a title for your drawing.

Discussion

• What activity, hobby, or interest sustains your mental health and wellness?

• Do you engage in this self-care activity frequently?

• How can you include this self-care activity, even for 10 to 15 minutes a day, in your weekly schedule?

• Is there a new self-care activity that you would like to practice in the future?

Supervision variation

First, supervisors introduce to supervisees the concept and signs of burn-out (i.e., feelings of emotional exhaustion, stress, and disengagement) (Freudenberger, 1975) and compassion fatigue (i.e., difficulty with concentration, productivity, and emotional presence) (Weiss, 2004). Then supervisees voice their past and current self-care activities and are invited to draw a picture of one of the activities they will focus on and engage in that will sustain their mental health and wellness during their academic and clinical internship journey.

Case example

Figure 5.2 illustrates a sustainable self drawing created by Marie (pseudonym), a psychotherapy student, depicting her self-care activity, that of journaling. The following presents Marie's expressive writing associated with her sustainable self drawing:

> Journaling is one of my artful expressions of choice, consistently serving as an effective medium for self-care. Slowing down mentally, by grounding myself in the here-and-now, is a needed practice within my daily life. As a thinker, I hold an insatiable desire to learn, creating a challenge within to allow my mind the time to simply relax. As such, journaling is a dependable outlet that, when practiced, yields internal calm and regulation to cognitive angst and somatic affect. Journaling provides reflective opportunity to share my deepest thoughts, reactions, ideas, dreams, fears, doubts, and victories, without the concern of outside judgment. Oftentimes, inner motivation ensues through this practice as I scribe big-picture ideas infiltrating my mind, leading to fresh aspirations in life... Through this artful medium, a release of pent-up emotions generally results, as I express myself through pen, onto the paper. Additionally, journaling is a peaceful act, creating space for me

to be in direct communion with that which I hold to be sacred, thereby replenishing my spirit. As such, the act of expressing words on paper, through my preferred art form of journaling, regularly brings a personal sense of holistic health and freedom.

The sustainable self arts activity permitted Marie to symbolically become mindful of her past and current journaling practice that disconnects her from career and life stressors, and rejuvenates her mind, body, and soul.

Figure 5.2 Sustainable self

5.5
VISUAL AFFIRMATIONS

Materials

Poster board, colored pens, colored post-it notes, glue, glitter glue, gems, rubber stamps.

Procedure

1. Note that affirmations are statements or phrases that enable individuals to think more positively about themselves and life.

2. With a colored pen, write positive statements about yourself on the post-it notes. The statements should be written in present tense and commence with "I am." For example, "I am a good friend." "I am able to make people laugh."

3. Add your positive statements to the vision board. As you attach each statement, say each statement out loud. Embellish your vision board in any way you like with the other art materials.

Discussion

• How does seeing and hearing your affirmations make you feel?

• What are you good at?

• What acts of kindness do you carry out for yourself and others?

Note

This activity can be administered at the end of each therapy session. Clients can write on a post-it note one affirmation statement per session and then add the statement to their vision board. During the final therapy session, clients are invited to read out loud all their affirmations. This activity enables clients to watch their visual affirmations grow!

○ Chapter 6 ○

GOALS

According to psychologist Robert Emmons (2003), a leader in the positive psychology movement, goals "are the concretized expression of future orientation and life purpose, and provide a convenient and powerful metric for examining these vital elements of a positive life" (p.106). Emmons further emphasized that establishing concrete short-term and long-term goals inspires individuals to grow, overcome life challenges, and move forward along their life journey. The inability to establish a goal mindset may lead one to struggle with "developmental paralysis" (Damon, 2009)—a period in their life when they are overwhelmed by feelings of emptiness, boredom, or being stuck.

Individuals often come to therapy complaining of feeling stuck along their life journey. Business psychologist Timothy Butler (2010) clarified that "being at impasse is a developmental necessity. It can lead to a new way of understanding and a new type of information" (p.2). Butler further emphasized that individuals remain developmentally stuck until they gain momentum towards new life pathways and future goals. Thus, one of the treatment objectives in therapy is to help clients become aware of the elements causing their developmental paralysis, commence envisioning future life pathways, and establish short-term goals that are linked to long-term goals.

Goal setting is a process by which individuals achieve their goals. Evan Locke and Gary Latham (1990) identified five elements that help individuals stay motivated and achieve effective goals. The first element is *clarity*—the goal needs to be clear and specific. The second element is *challenge*—the goal should be challenging yet realistic and attainable. The third element is *commitment*—individuals need to be interested in achieving the goal. The fourth element is *feedback*—the goal needs to be measurable so individuals can see their progress. The final element is *task complexity*—if individuals find their goal too large or complicated, then they should break down the goal to smaller sub-goals.

The following arts activities help clients establish a future and goal mindset, and identify important short-term and long-term goals, as well as resources that will assist them with overcoming obstacles that stand in their way of achieving their goals. A number of these arts activities are built on Paul Wong's (2012) "double-vision" therapeutic approach aimed at addressing individuals' short-term goals and long-term goals. The arts activities are well suited to clients who are struggling with developmental paralysis and prepared to move forward along their life journey. Additionally, these arts activities can be administered to clients who are physically and psychologically preparing to undergo transition. For example, adolescents shifting into higher education or the workforce; adults who are incarcerated or temporarily residing in a residential addiction center and are about to transition back into society; and adolescents and adults who have recently immigrated to a new country.

6.1
GETTING UNSTUCK

Materials

Colored markers or pencils, pen, *Getting unstuck activity sheet* (see Appendix J).

Procedure

1. Note that there are moments in our lives when we find ourselves stuck, unable to move forward towards the future.

2. Copy the *Getting unstuck activity sheet*.

3. Reflect on two or three moments in your life when you metaphorically felt stuck. With a pen or colored marker, on the inside of the shoe image, write down the moments when you were stuck, and on the outside of the shoe, write or draw symbols depicting the elements (i.e., people, places, and things) that helped you get unstuck.

Discussion

- What elements (i.e., people, places, and things) helped you get unstuck in the past?

- What, or who, sparks movement in you?

- What affirmations—positive thoughts and feelings—motivate you to keep moving forward?

- Are you currently feeling stuck? If yes, what simple act can help you become unstuck?

- What motivates you to get up every morning?

Supervision variation

Supervisors prompt supervisees to reflect on clinical cases that they are stuck on and develop strategies that will assist them with moving forward with the challenging cases.

6.2
BRIDGE DRAWING WITH PATH (BDP)

Materials

Drawing paper, colored markers, colored pencils, pencil, pen. 3D option: cardboard, construction paper, craft sticks, tape, scissors, clay, pipe cleaners.

Procedure

1. Draw a bridge from someplace to someplace. The bridge connects to a path. Draw the path and write or say where it leads you to.

2. Once finished, provide a title for your image.

Discussion

*   Where is your path leading you to?

*   Does your path lead to a crossroad? If yes, which paths are ahead of you? Which path is brighter and more hopeful?

*   Who, or what, will keep you motivated to reach the pathway endpoint or goal?

*   Did you depict yourself in the drawing? If yes, are you on the bridge or the path?

Group sculpture variation

Therapists facilitating groups could prompt group members to build a 3D bridge connecting to a path using recycled and found objects. Once finished, group members collectively determine and discuss where the path is leading them to.

Supervision variation

Supervisors can administer the bridge drawing with path activity during closure sessions for supervisees to pause and reflect upon the knowledge and skills they have gained from their training program and how their clinical field placement has morphed their career goals and professional identity.

Note

The *Bridge drawing with path rating scale* (Darewych, 2013) can be used when administering the activity as an assessment tool in clinical or research settings (see Appendix K) and can be coupled with the Adult State Hope Scale (ASHS) (Snyder *et al.*, 1996), also known as the Goal Scale, and the Meaning in Life Questionnaire (MLQ) (Steger *et al.*, 2006) (Darewych, 2014; Darewych & Brown Campbell, 2016).

Case example

Figure 6.1 displays a bridge drawing with path created by Evan (pseudonym), a young adult with high-functioning autism, during a single study session investigating imagination in adults with ASD (Darewych *et al.*, 2018). Evan drew a local top-arched bridge that crossed over water and connected to two paths. The left path led to one city where he lived, while the right path led to another city where he attended his daily programs. Evan also drew boats under the bridge floating on the water. During the session, Evan had an opportunity to verbally describe the programs he enjoyed participating in during the week and the people, places, and things he saw along his journey across the local bridge.

Figure 6.1 Bridge drawing with path

6.3
CAREER ANCHORS

Materials

Poster board, magazine images, colored markers, glitter glue, found objects, *Career anchors activity sheet* (see Appendix L). 3D option: multi-colored air-drying clay, acrylic paint.

Procedure

1. Note that career anchors are the distinguished talents, needs, and values that shape an individual's career identity. The examination of personal career anchors can assist individuals with clarifying their career directions, goals, and settings (Schein, 1978).

2. Copy the *Career anchors activity sheet* and then cut the anchor shape out.

3. With the anchor cut-out, create a mixed-media collage that symbolically depicts your professional talents, needs, and values.

4. Once finished, provide a title for your mixed-media career anchors collage.

Discussion

- What special talents and skills will you bring to your chosen work field?

- What resources can help you achieve your career goals?

- What do you hope your career will provide you with or allow you to do?

- Which career setting(s) do you believe matches your personal and professional values the best?

- What new career-related skills and talents would you like to develop in the near future?

Supervision variation

Supervisors can administer the career anchors activity during the early stages of supervision for supervisees to reflect on their current skills and talents that they can use to facilitate therapeutic sessions and establish therapeutic alliances with their clients. The activity can also be used during closure supervision sessions for supervisees to pause and reflect on the knowledge and skills they gained from their training program and how their clinical field placement experience has morphed into their career goals and identity.

Note

For further reading on the career anchors arts activity, see Darewych (2019).

6.4
FUTURE TRIP

Materials

Drawing paper, colored markers or pencils.

Procedure

1. Imagine you are going on a trip next week.

2. With the materials provided, draw the place you would like to visit.

3. Once finished, provide a title for your drawing.

Discussion

- Where would you like to travel?

- What, or who, would you take with you?

- Is this a place where you have traveled to in the past?

- What is the purpose of your travels or adventure? To relax? Explore a new place? Accomplish a goal?

Note

Therapists can use the *Future trip drawing rating scale* (Darewych, 2015 when administering this activity as an arts-based assessment tool in clinical or research settings (see Appendix M).

Case example

Figure 6.2 displays a future trip drawing created by Matthew (pseudonym), a young adult with high-functioning autism, during a single study session investigating imagination in adults with ASD (Darewych *et al.*, 2018). Matthew divided his drawing paper into three sections and drew three places he would like to visit. The first was the "Empire State Building in New York City." The second place was "Warner Brothers Studio" in California. And the third place was the "Dan Marino Foundation for people with autism," which is located in Florida. Matthew titled his drawing "Dream Vacation." During the session, Matthew briefly reflected on whether his travel goals were realistic and possible.

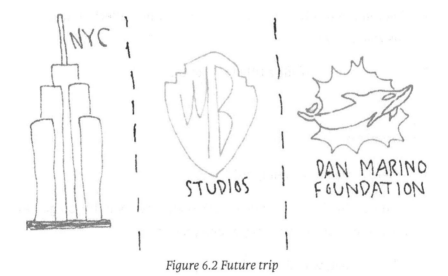

Figure 6.2 Future trip

6.5
BUS TO FUTURE

Materials

Colored markers or pencils, *Bus to future activity sheet* (see Appendix N).

Procedure

1. Copy the *Bus to future activity sheet*.

2. Color in the bus to the future. While coloring, reflect on where the bus will take you.

3. Once finished, provide a title for your drawing.

Discussion

- Where is the bus traveling to?

- If you could climb into the driver's seat, where would you go next week, one month from now, or one year from now?

- Who, or what, would you take with you?

- Are there people or things that you will not allow on the bus?

- Is this a place where you have traveled to in the past?

6.6
TIME CAPSULE

Materials

Miniature glass capsule or bead container, origami paper, glitter, stars, gel pens.

Procedure

1. Note that establishing goals helps individuals to achieve their hopes and desires.

2. Take a moment to reflect on a goal you would like to achieve within a short period of time (i.e., within one week, two weeks, or one month).

3. With a colored gel pen, write your short-term goal on a small sheet of rectangular origami paper.

4. When you finish writing down your goal, roll up the paper with your goal and then insert the paper in the miniature capsule.

5. Place the miniature capsule which holds your short-term goal in a place where you will come across it in the very near future so that you can determine if you achieved your short-term goal. If you do not accomplish your short-term goal during the determined timeframe, then place the time capsule where it is visible as a reminder to accomplish your goal.

Discussion

• What short-term goal do you want to achieve in one month?

• Is your short-term goal realistic and attainable?

- Why do you want to achieve your short-term goal?

- What do you need to do during the next few days or weeks to achieve your short-term goal?

- Do any obstacles stand in your way from achieving your short-term goal? If yes, what are the inner and outer resources and character strengths that will assist you with overcoming the obstacles?

- How will you feel when you have achieved your short-term goal?

- How can you celebrate your achievement?

- Is your short-term goal connected to a long-term goal? If yes, how is your short-term goal connected to the long-term goal?

- What long-term goal do you want to achieve in one year, two years, or five years?

- Is this a personal goal or a goal dictated by others?

- What other short-term or long-term goals would you like to achieve?

Supervision variation

Supervisors can administer this arts activity during the first supervision session for supervisees to creatively explore and discuss goals that they hope to achieve from their supervision journey or clinical internship experiences.

Simple modification

Therapists can simplify this arts activity for clients who currently have no goal in mind by directing them to explore a modest goal that they would like to achieve by the end of the day or tomorrow.

Chapter 7

MEANING

People throughout their lives search for meaning and purpose. Finding meaning in life is a basic human need that brings individuals psychological stability in our current hectic world (Baumeister & Vohs, 2010). The grand existential question of "What is the meaning of my life?" is often difficult to answer even for individuals who are flourishing and functioning well. Psychologist Michael Steger (2012), from the Laboratory for the Study of Meaning and Quality of Life at Colorado State University, defined meaning as "the web of connections, understandings, and interpretations that help us comprehend our experience and formulate plans directing energies to the achievement of our desired future" (p.165). Studies investigating the concept of meaning have found that individuals with higher levels of meaning report more future directions (Steger *et al.*, 2008), higher levels of hope (Steger *et al.*, 2006), and lower levels of depression and anxiety (Mascaro & Rosen, 2006). Individuals who struggle to achieve a personal sense of a meaningful life succumb to an "existential vacuum"—a time and space filled with feelings of inner emptiness, hopelessness, and loneliness (Frankl, 1946 [2006]).

Over several decades now, mental health professionals have emphasized that the creative process, in and of itself, can reduce individuals' feelings of emptiness and illuminate sources that provide them with life meanings (Allen, 2005; da Silva, 2005; Frankl, 1986; Lantz, 1993). Moreover, Csikszentmihályi (1996) proclaimed "creativity is a central source of meaning in our lives" (p.1), and Allen (2005) deemed art as a path to meaning. Studies examining the concept of meaning have identified the following as primary sources that provide individuals with a sense of life meaning: significant relationships, career and academic achievements, belonging to community organizations, spirituality, and self-development (Damon, 2009; Darewych, 2014; Steger *et al.*, 2013).

The following arts activities invite clients to focus on the present moment and explore the daily sources (i.e., people, places, and things) that give them meaning and purpose in life.

7.1
SOURCES OF MEANING

Materials

Magazine images depicting colors, nature, objects, symbols, and people.

Procedure

1. Take a few minutes to visually explore the magazine images in front of you.

2. Now select one image showing colors, nature, objects, symbols, and people that make your life feel meaningful.

3. After you have selected your image, on a sheet of paper, or in your journal book, write down, in a free association style, all the elements (i.e., people, places, and things) that fill your mind, body, and soul with life meaning.

Discussion

- Describe the image you selected.

- What element(s) is/are depicted in the image?

- What does meaning mean to you?

- How does this/these element(s) bring meaning to your life?

Note

The sources of meaning activity could be paired with the Meaning in Life Questionnaire (MLQ) (Steger *et al.*, 2006) or the Flourishing Scale (Diener *et al.*, 2009).

For further reading on sources of meaning arts activities, see Darewych and Riedel Bowers (2017) and Steger *et al.* (2013).

7.2
DOWNWARD AND UPWARD SPIRAL

Materials

Colored markers or pencils, scissors, and *Downward and upward spiral activity sheet* (see Appendix O).

Procedure

1. Copy the *Downward and upward spiral activity sheet*.

2. Cut the spiral out and then place the spiral on the table in front of you.

3. On one side of the spiral, write down and add symbols representing the elements (i.e., people, places, and things) that trigger negative emotions and make you spiral downward. On reflecting on the elements on your downward spiral, flip the spiral, and on the other side, write down and add symbols representing the elements that elicit positive emotions, bring meaning to your life, and make you spiral upward.

Discussion

- What elements trigger negative emotions, make your life feel meaningless, and make you spiral downward?

- What elements elicit positive emotions, make your life feel meaningful, and make you spiral upward?

7.3
LIVING IN THE PRESENT—
MARKETPLACE

Materials

Living in the present—marketplace photograph and activity sheet (see Appendices P & Q).

Procedure

1. Copy the marketplace photograph and marketplace coloring outline template.

2. Take a moment to visually connect with the marketplace photograph.

3. While viewing the marketplace photograph, read the following corresponding marketplace short story:

   A market is where people gather to buy or sell or trade many different items, often food. It can be both indoors or outdoors, and can operate daily or weekly depending on population and culture. Markets have existed for thousands of years, ever since people have been engaged in trade, and likely originated in the Middle East, where a bazaar was typically arranged in long strips with stalls on either side, and a covered roof intended to protect the buyers and sellers from the hot sun. Daily shopping at a market can be a way of life in many cultures. Designated marketplaces have become important sites of historic and architectural significance, and some cities consider their markets to be a major cultural asset, as well as a popular tourist destination. In recent years, Farmers Markets have become very popular with a growing desire to encourage and support a local food movement. (Zeller Cooper, 2019, para. 1)

4. Once you have finished reading, color in the marketplace outline template.

Discussion

- What is under the market tent?

- What is in one of the baskets?

- What color are the baskets?

- What are the different shapes of the baskets?

- Why is the tent up?

- What is at the bottom left corner of the picture?

- What is the person doing?

Note

The living in the present—marketplace activity was developed by psychotherapist and art therapist Esther Zeller Cooper (2019) for older adults with or without dementia. Her *Living in the Present* manual consists of vibrant and colorful images depicting simple yet mature subject matter which visually challenge older adults to use their present imaginative thinking abilities without having to focus on past memories or future visions. The objective of the arts activity is for older adults, in an individual or group setting, to engage in a here-and-now activity that allows them to gain a sense of accomplishment and awareness of meaningful moments in their present lives.

7.4
LABYRINTH WALK

Materials

Outdoor labyrinth, journal book.

Procedure

1. Note that a labyrinth is a circular path that leads the walker to a center point. It is not a maze, and its shape symbolizes the twists and turns of an individual's life journey. One can find a labyrinth in nature, in churches, and in common city spaces. Walking a labyrinth, slowly and with a set intention, enables an individual to focus, become mindful of their breath and steps, and envision the meaningful elements (i.e., people, places, and things) in their life.

2. Take a moment to walk a labyrinth. Before you commence walking the inward path, set your journal book and writing instrument by the entrance of the labyrinth, and determine your set intention for walking the labyrinth (e.g., connecting with meaningful sources). When you reach the center of the labyrinth, spend two to five minutes at the center point and deeply focus on the present and meaningful source(s) (i.e., people, places, and things) you are envisioning and connecting with.

3. When ready, begin to walk the outward path. As you walk out of the labyrinth, pick up your journal book and writing instrument and begin to write down the meaningful sources that you envisioned as you walked the labyrinth, specifically the meaningful source(s) that you envisioned and connected with in the center of the labyrinth.

Discussion

- What meaningful source(s) did you envision and connect with while walking the labyrinth?

- What meaningful source(s) did you envision and connect with at the center of the labyrinth?

- What other thoughts and feelings came to mind while walking in and out of the labyrinth?

Indoor variation

The therapist can invite clients to walk the paper-based *Labyrinth activity sheet* (see Appendix R) using their finger. This paper-based finger labyrinth activity can be used as a warm-up activity to help clients who are agitated and anxious to disconnect from life stressors and calm their state of mind.

○ Chapter 8 ○

SPIRITUALITY

Spirituality is a mysterious element of individuals' lives. The concept of spirituality is becoming more readily explored and applied in the field of positive psychology and psychotherapy. Psychologist Kenneth Pargament (2007), a leading scholar in spiritually integrated psychotherapy, exclaimed that individuals can find the spiritual "in a piece of music, the smile of a passing stranger, the color of the sky at dusk, or a daily prayer of gratitude upon awakening" (p.3). Similarly, Thomas Plante (2008) emphasized that activities such as meditation, prayer, ritual, and sacred connections enable individuals in psychotherapy to establish deeper spirituality and explore spiritual pathways and sources. Individuals do not have to be religious to be spiritual and to engage in such spiritual practices (Fuller, 2001). Such spiritual practices, experiences, and relationships are correlated with happiness, hope, meaning in life, and well-being (Koenig, McCullough, & Larson, 2001).

In therapy, spirituality is often a source of hope for clients undergoing an "existential vacuum" (Frankl, 1986)—a period in their lives when they are flooded by feelings of hopelessness, emptiness, and isolation. During the therapeutic journey, clients may consciously not be aware that they are exploring spiritual experiences, pathways, sources, or struggles. As a result, therapists must turn on their "spiritual radars," use spiritual language, and become attuned to spiritual words such as peace, solace, faith, hope, love, letting go, forgiveness, despair, and suffering (Griffith & Griffith, 2002; Pargament, 2007). Moreover, the therapeutic space can be perceived as a sacred space; a space where clients, in the presence of a therapist, gain a sense of safety, work through unresolved issues, share their deepest secrets or trauma survivor stories, undergo change, and gain wisdom.

Pargament (2007) underscored that it is a challenge for individuals to articulate their spirituality in words, and as a result of this he suggests that individuals explore their sacred pathways, sources, and spaces in visual form via symbols and metaphors. Art therapist Pat Allen (2005) claimed that the making and viewing of art, in and of itself, can be a spiritual experience.

The following arts activities prompt clients to reflect on spirituality, explore spiritual pathways, sources, and struggles, reconnect with spiritual practices and beliefs, search for the sacred, and commence a spiritual quest. Therapists can couple these arts activities with the spiritual pathway assessment (Ortberg & Barton, 2001).

8.1
SACRED SINGING BOWL

Materials

Tibetan or Himalayan instrumental music. Option: Tibetan or Himalayan singing bowl with wooden striker.

Procedure

1. Note that, for centuries, Tibetan and Himalayan singing bowls have been used for meditative purposes.

2. Sit comfortably in your chair with your feet planted flat on the ground and your hands placed flat on your thighs. For five to ten minutes, close your eyes. Concentrate on your breathing and relax your mind while you listen to the rich, deep tone of the singing bowl.

3. When ready, open your eyes and return to the room.

Discussion

- What other sounds or music calm your state of mind?

- What does meditation mean to you?

- What ways do you meditate?

- Do you engage in any spiritual rituals or practices? If yes, where?

Note

Therapists can play Tibetan or Himalayan music as a warm-up and closing session activity for clients to calm their state of mind.

8.2
SACRED SPACE

Materials

Drawing paper, oil or soft pastels. Option: watercolor paper and watercolor paint.

Procedure

1. Sit comfortably in your chair. With your eyes open or closed, begin visualizing a sacred space in your life where you physically and psychologically disconnect from external stressors and gain a sense of peace. Visualize the details of this space, including the sights, sounds, and smells.

2. When ready, using colors, shapes, and forms, draw your sacred space.

3. Once finished, provide a title for your drawing.

Discussion

- What, or where, is your sacred space?

- What sensory objects exist in your sacred space?

- Do you visit your sacred space frequently?

- What does spirituality mean to you?

- What are your spiritual beliefs and values?

- Do you believe in any mysterious, higher power forces?

- Are you a member of a spiritual community or group?

- Is there a spiritual community or group you would like to belong to in the future?

Note

The word "sacred" may not resonate with all clients, especially for those who have been harmed spiritually. Instead, therapists can direct clients to draw a special space or place.

8.3
SPIRITUAL PATHWAY

Materials

Photographs or magazine images of pathways through nature.

Procedure

1. View the photograph depicting a spiritual path meandering through a meadow or brightly lit forest.

Discussion

- Where is the pathway leading you?

- What does spirituality mean to you?

- What are your spiritual beliefs and values?

- Do you believe in any mysterious, higher power forces?

- Are you a member of a spiritual community or group?

- Is there a spiritual community or group you would like to belong to in the future?

Note

The spiritual pathway endpoint may illuminate the client's spiritual story, sacred source, or sacred place. The pathway endpoint can be compared to

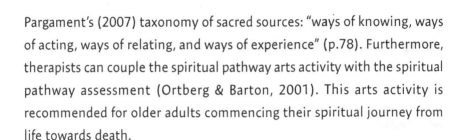

Pargament's (2007) taxonomy of sacred sources: "ways of knowing, ways of acting, ways of relating, and ways of experience" (p.78). Furthermore, therapists can couple the spiritual pathway arts activity with the spiritual pathway assessment (Ortberg & Barton, 2001). This arts activity is recommended for older adults commencing their spiritual journey from life towards death.

8.4
PORTABLE ALTAR

Materials

Cardboard or tin box, construction paper, tissue paper, magazine images, beads, feathers, glitter, and found objects such as scented candles and crystals.

Procedure

1. Take a moment to gather your thoughts and establish a calm state of mind.

2. With the materials provided, create a miniature portable altar that you will be able to take with you anywhere to establish a sacred place where you can perform a ritual, read a spiritual book, contemplate, meditate, pray, and visualize your favorite kind of day or a beautiful day.

Discussion

*   Describe your miniature portable altar.

*   What objects exist in your miniature portable altar?

*   Where will you place or take it?

*   When will you visit your miniature portable altar?

*   What does meditation mean to you?

- What ways do you meditate?

- What does spirituality mean to you?

- What are your spiritual beliefs and values?

- Do you believe in any mysterious, higher power forces?

- Are you a member of a spiritual community or group?

- Is there a spiritual community or group you would like to belong to in the future?

Note

This arts activity is well suited to clients who are isolated from society and physically separated from their traditional sacred spaces, communities, and groups; for example, older adults residing in long-term care facilities and adolescents and adults residing in residential centers or mental health facilities.

8.5
THREE BLESSINGS

Materials

Writing paper, pencil, pen, or fine colored markers.

Procedure

1. On a piece of paper, with your writing instrument, write down three good things that happened to you today.

Discussion

- What went well today?

- What did not go well?

- What needs to change to make things better in your life?

Note

This writing activity is based on the three good things activity (Seligman *et al.*, 2005).

8.6
PRAYER FLAGS

Materials

Small rectangular canvas or felt piece (approx. 9" x 12"), fabric markers, hanging string, yarn, thread, beads, stamps, scissors, glue, hole puncher.

Procedure

1. Note that prayer flags are believed to have originated in Tibet. They were hung along mountain walking trails in the Himalayan mountains to bless the surrounding land and people and to send messages of goodwill to the world.

2. With the materials provided, create a prayer flag that will bless you, your surroundings, and the people around you. In the center of your prayer flag, write a prayer, a sacred poem, or a goodwill message to the world. You can also add sacred colors, symbols, and images to your prayer flag.

3. Hang or pin the prayer flag in your sacred space.

Discussion

- Describe your prayer flag.

- What is written and depicted on your prayer flag?

- What does it mean for you to pray?

- Where, or how, do you pray?

8.7
GIFT OF FORGIVENESS

Materials

Mixed-media.

Procedure

1. Note that forgiveness is a means of coping with distress after being harmed by another person. Certain individuals who have been physically and/or psychologically wounded by another person often struggle with forgiving the other's hurtful actions. The act of forgiving has the ability to reduce feelings of anger and increase feelings of optimism (Worthington, 2001).

2. Create a gift of forgiveness for a person you would like to forgive for their hurtful actions. The gift could be a letter, poem, or song of forgiveness.

3. Deliver the gift of forgiveness to the person.

Discussion

- How did the person harm you?

- Are you prepared to forgive the person?

- What gift of forgiveness have you created for the person?

Note

Forgiveness is also an important character strength under the virtue of temperance (see Chapter 4).

8.8
SACRED ANIMAL

Materials

Drawing paper, colored markers or pencils, soft pastels. 3D option: soft clay or plasticine.

Procedure

1. Take a moment to reflect on what you believe is your sacred animal.

2. Draw or sculpt your sacred animal.

3. Once finished, name your sacred animal.

Discussion

• What sacred animal did you depict?

• What does your sacred animal protect you from?

• What strengths does your sacred animal hold?

• Which natural surroundings would you like to visit in the future?

8.9
NATURE WALK

Materials

Natural surroundings.

Procedure

1. Take a moment in your life to sit on a park bench or stroll along a park path. Make a special effort to actively savor and appreciate your natural surroundings. Admire the beauty that surrounds you and observe the forces of nature that shift around you. Gaze up at the sky and watch the clouds float over you. Feel the gentle breeze, feel the sun's warmth, and smell the flowers.

Discussion

- What blissful or meaningful experiences have you had with nature in the past?

- Which natural surroundings would you like to visit in the future?

- Do you consider nature a sacred or special place?

○ Chapter 9 ○

WELL-BEING

As highlighted at the beginning of this book, positive psychology is also known as the science of well-being. Psychologist Carol Ryff (1989) devised a theoretical model of psychological well-being which outlines six dimensions that contribute to individuals' mental health and wellness: autonomy, environmental mastery, personal growth, positive relations with others, purpose in life, and self-acceptance. Two decades later, Martin Seligman (2011) developed the PERMA model, which delineates five aspects that contribute to individuals' well-being: positive emotions, engagement, relationships, meaning, and achievement. Research has shown that individuals with higher levels of psychological well-being tend to have the capacity to make autonomous decisions, undergo personal growth, unceasingly control and connect with their environment, establish healthy relationships with others within multiple contexts (e.g., education, family, work), gain a sense of meaning in life, and acknowledge their multiple self-aspects (Ryff, 1989; Ryff & Keyes, 1995).

Previous chapters in this book described arts activities that enable individuals to express positive emotions (see Chapter 3), gain insight to their multiple aspects of self (see Chapter 5) reflect on personal goals (see Chapter 6), and explore sources of meaning (see Chapter 7). This chapter specifically describes arts activities related to aspects from

Ryff's (1989) and Seligman's (2011) models of well-being that enable individuals to make independent decisions, reconnect with their natural surroundings, build positive relationships in group settings, and reflect on sources of well-being.

9.1
ALL ON MY OWN

Materials

Drawing paper, colored markers or pencils.

Procedure

1. Draw a picture of yourself engaged in an activity or task that you recently accomplished on your own without support from others.

2. Once finished, provide a title for your drawing.

Discussion

*   Describe your drawing.

*   What activity did you accomplish on your own?

*   Which character strengths did you use to accomplish this activity?

*   How did you feel when you accomplished this activity?

*   How can you celebrate your achievement?

9.2
NATURE SCULPT

Materials

Objects found in nature: driftwood, sand, sticks, stones, shells, coral, leaves, seaweed, grasses.

Procedure

1. Explore and shape the nature-based materials. Bring a moment of peacefulness to your life.

Discussion

- What nature-based objects did you use to create your sculpture?

- Which sensory materials did you like best?

- Do you connect with nature frequently?

- Which natural surroundings do you find peaceful?

Case example

Figure 9.1 illustrates a 3D nature sculpture created by youth orphans (aged 12–18) in Ukraine during a one-hour strengths-based group art therapy session which occurred outdoors in a natural beach setting. Group members were prompted to create a sand sculpture using found objects from the natural beach setting symbolically representing humor, one of the VIA 24 character strengths (Peterson & Seligman, 2004). This particular group collectively chose to create a sand sculpture using beach sand, shells, and sandstones to depict a clown. Near the end of the sculpting process, two members of the group requested acrylic paint in order to add color to the shells and sandstones. During the post-activity group dialogue, group members reflected on their recent adventure to see a circus, and how the clowns' silly performance acts made them laugh and uplifted their spirits.

The group art therapy session which occurred outdoors permitted the youth orphans, who predominantly reside in orphanages located in or near an industrial city with minimal green space, the opportunity to gain a sense of appreciation of nature and reconnect with the natural beach setting using their senses. More specifically, the nature sculpt arts activity encouraged the youth orphans during the group process to utilize their character strengths of creativity, social intelligence, and team work, and express the character strength of humor verbally and non-verbally in a creative way.

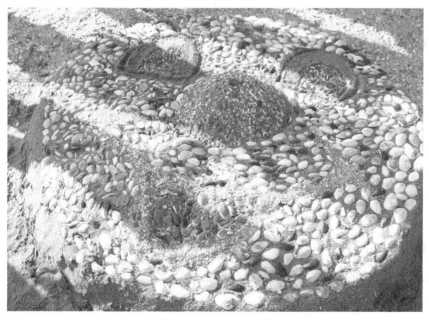

Figure 9.1 Nature sculpt

9.3
INTERACTIVE DRAWING TASK (IDT)

Materials

Drawing paper, colored markers or pencils.

Procedure

1. Draw a picture with the other person. The two of you can talk during the interactive drawing process. Together, decide what colors, shapes, and symbols to draw. One rule is not to draw over the other person's shapes or symbols.

2. When finished, provide a title for your drawing.

Discussion

- What did the two of you decide to draw?

- What was it like to draw together on one sheet of paper?

- Did you support the other person in any way?

- What is the title of your drawing?

Note

The interactive drawing task was developed by Backer van Ommeren *et al.* (2015). The activity encourages clients in a group setting to interact and create with other group members. In therapeutic sessions, the interactive drawing task can be used by the therapist to assess each group member's openness and social ability to interact with others.

Supervision variation

Supervisors could administer the interactive drawing task as a fun creative activity at the early stages of the supervision journey to establish rapport with supervisees.

9.4
ISLAND OF CONNECTIVITY

Materials

Large drawing paper (18" x 24"), colored markers or pencils.

Procedure

1. The therapist reads the following solution-focused scenario about being stranded on an island:

   You are all on a boat that has struck an obstacle in the water that has caused some damage to the boat. There is an island nearby that everyone can swim to with their life jackets on. As a group, you are able to take five items and a sack of food to the island with you for survival purposes until the rescue team arrives. On the island, there is a waterfall and a cluster of fruit trees. As a group, determine who will build temporary shelter from the sun and wind, and which individuals will prepare food. Additionally, determine actions to quicken your rescue. (Darewych, in press)

2. As a group, draw or build your island.

3. Finally, name your island.

Discussion

- What was it like to engage in a creative activity with others?

- Which character strengths and interpersonal skills did you use during the group activity in order to work with and support others?

- Did the group come across any challenging moments during the activity? If yes, what were they, and how did the group work together to overcome the challenges?

- Who in the group encouraged and motivated others?

- Identify a character strength in one of the group members.

9.5
WELLNESS CONTAINER

Materials

Shoe box with lid, paint sticks, magazine images, buttons, gems, glitter, rubber stamps, personal wellness items (e.g., favorite music CDs, photographs, herbal tea bags, scented candles).

Procedure

1. Paint the outside of the box and lid with colors that you believe are calming. Using other art materials, embellish the outside of the box in any way. Place items in the box from your current life surroundings that provide you with a sense of comfort, harmony, and balance. For example, affirmation statements, favorite music CDs, photographs, magazine images, self-help books, scented candles.

Discussion

- Describe your wellness container.

- What items did you place in your wellness container?

- Which positive emotions, character strengths, and sources of meaning can you use to establish a healthy, balanced, good life?

- What are your current mental health and wellness goals?

- Are there any obstacles currently preventing you from achieving your mental health and wellness goals? If yes, what are they, and how can you overcome them?

○ Chapter 10 ○

CONCLUSION

To this day, the arts such as dance, drama, drawing, music, poetry, and storytelling continue to be used by individuals of all ages across cultures and nations as healing practices, forms of self-expression, and pathways towards transformation. Consequently, mental health professionals are increasingly integrating the arts in their clinical practice as creative tools to promote the physical, psychological, social, and spiritual well-being of their clients.

This book has presented a number of action-oriented and reflective positive psychology arts activities that mental health professionals can integrate into their therapeutic sessions. These activities are creative vehicles through which individuals can explore creative outlets, engage in the act of flow, express negative and positive emotions, identify character strengths, undergo self-awareness, gain insight to personal goals, reflect on sources of life meaning, discover spirituality, and cultivate well-being.

While these positive psychology arts activities can be a catalyst for positive growth and transformation, they also have the ability to tap into clients' repressed negative emotions, defenses, and unresolved issues. Thus, it is important that mental health professionals who are interested in integrating these positive psychology arts activities into their clinical practice gain competencies in clinical arts approaches.

A number of accredited creative arts therapies programs exist in Australia, Asia, Canada, Europe, and the United States that provide formal training and professional workshops in clinical arts approaches.

The positive psychology arts activities featured in this book are still in need of empirical support; thus I call on researchers in the field of creative arts therapies and positive psychology to jointly investigate the effects and benefits of these arts activities on individuals' mental health and well-being in clinical settings. Future studies could administer a number of these arts activities in parallel with self-report questionnaires developed by scholars in the field of positive psychology that assess the same concept (see Table 10.1).

For the reader who is interested in expanding their positive psychology arts activities toolbox even further, I recommend reading Wilkinson and Chilton's (2018) book entitled *Positive Art Therapy Theory and Practice*. Wilkinson and Chilton present a number of positive art therapy directives such as Golden Moments, Love Map, and Strengths Mobile in the appendix section of their book. And for the reader who is interested in learning more about positive supervision, I recommend Bannink's (2015) book entitled *Handbook of Positive Supervision*.

Table 10.1 Positive psychology arts activities with supplementary self-report questionnaires

Positive psychology concepts	Arts activities	Self-report questionnaires
Imagination	Scribble drawing	Hunter Imagination Questionnaire (Jung, Flores, & Hunter, 2016)
Flow	Zesty flow	Flow State Scale (Jackson & Marsh, 1996)

Character strengths	Strengths collage Tree of Life	VIA 24 Character Strengths Questionnaire (Peterson & Seligman, 2004)
Goals	Bridge drawing with path	Adult State Hope Scale (Snyder et al., 1996) Meaning in Life Questionnaire (Steger et al., 2006)
Positive emotions: Gratitude Hope	My favorite kind of day Gratitude scroll Hope ritual	Subjective Happiness Questionnaire (Lyubomirsky & Lepper, 1999) Gratitude Questionnaire (McCullough et al., 2002) Adult State Hope Scale (Snyder et al., 1996)
Meaning	Sources of meaning	Meaning in Life Questionnaire (Steger et al., 2006)
Spirituality	Spiritual pathway	Spiritual Pathway Assessment (Ortberg & Barton, 2001)
Well-being	All of my own interactive drawing task Wellness container	Flourishing Scale (Diener et al., 2009) Scale of Psychological Well-Being (Ryff, 1989)

Appendices

The appendices are available to download from https://library.jkp.com/ redeem using the code PAUNEZE

APPENDIX B: SPONTANEOUS SCRIBBLE ACTIVITY SHEET (Source: Darewych)

APPENDIX C: SCRIBBLE DRAWING RATING SCALE (2017, revised 2018. Source: Darewych, 2017a)

Image characteristics/variables

1. **Axis of the paper:** Indicate the axis of the paper.

   Code 0 for horizontal axis

   Code 1 for vertical axis

   Code 2 for undefined.

2. **Scribble transformation:** Indicate if scribble materialized into a symbol (i.e., person, place, or object).

   Code 0 for no transformation

   Code 1 for transformation into a symbol (i.e., person, place, or object).

3. **Symbol type:** Indicate type of symbol.

   Code 0 for person

   Code 1 for place

   Code 2 for object

   Code 3 for more than one symbol

   Code 4 for undefined.

4. **Written association tense (if applicable):**

   Code 0 for past tense

   Code 1 for present tense

   Code 2 for future tense

   Code 3 for multiple tenses.

Note: Permission is granted to use this rating scale for clinical and research purposes.

APPENDIX D: TRINITY CELTIC ART MANDALYNTH ACTIVITY SHEET (Source: Rado)

APPENDIX E: POSITIVITY PALETTE ACTIVITY SHEET (Source: Darewych)

APPENDIX F: GRATITUDE
SCROLL ACTIVITY SHEET
(Source: Microsoft Word Symbol)

APPENDIX G: CIRCLE ACTIVITY
SHEET (Source: Microsoft Word Symbol)

APPENDIX H: TREE OF LIFE ACTIVITY SHEET (Source: Darewych)

APPENDIX I: NESTING DOLL
ACTIVITY SHEET (Source: Darewych)

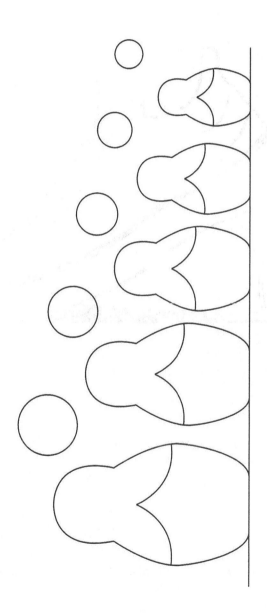

APPENDIX J: GETTING UNSTUCK
ACTIVITY SHEET (Source: Kuzmich)

APPENDIX K: BRIDGE DRAWING WITH PATH RATING SCALE (January 2013, revised 2015. Based on Hays & Lyons' (1981) bridge drawing. Source: Darewych, 2014)

Image characteristics/variables:

1. **Axis of the paper:** Indicate the axis of the paper.

   Code 0 for horizontal axis

   Code 1 for vertical axis

   Code 2 for undefined.

2. **Directionality:** Indicate the direction of the image as a whole.

   Code 0 for direction from left to right

   Code 1 for direction from right to left

   Code 2 for undefined; no movement left or right; centralized.

3. **Path quadrant:** Indicate if the *path drawn with written association* is located in the left quadrant, right quadrant, or omitted.

   Code 0 if path in the left quadrant

   Code 1 if path drawn in the right

   Code 2 if path drawn in the center

   Code 3 if path omitted

   Code 4 if left and right paths.

4. **Placement of self in the picture:** Indicate if person depicts self in picture.

   Code 0 for no self

   Code 1 if self is depicted in picture.

5. **Bridge connection:** Indicate if bridge floating or attached to land mass.

   Code 0 if bridge floating; not attached to land mass

   Code 1 if bridge attached to land mass

   Code 2 if bridge omitted.

6. **Bridge type:** Indicate the type of bridge depicted, e.g., arch or non-arch.

   Code 0 for non-arch type bridge

   Code 1 for arch type bridge

   Code 2 if bridge omitted.

7. **Matter drawn under bridge:** Indicate the matter drawn under bridge.

   Code 0 for none

   Code 1 for water—H_2O

   Code 2 for land.

8. **Written associations to the drawing:** Indicate the words, phrases, places, and themes written on the path/picture.

   Code 0 for home

Code 1 for family/friends

Code 2 for nature/forest

Code 3 for city/country

Code 4 for career

Code 5 for academic/education

Code 6 for future

Code 7 for spirituality, e.g., Heaven–Hell; to God; sacred sources/ places

Code 8 for opportunities

Code 9 for unknown/somewhere

Code 10 for other

Code 11 for no comment/none.

Optional: Indicate tense of written association.

Code 0 for present/here and now tense

Code 1 for past tense

Code 2 for future tense.

Note: Permission is granted to use this rating scale for clinical and research purposes. See Darewych (2014) for the full BDP Training Manual.

APPENDIX L: CAREER ANCHORS
ACTIVITY SHEET (Source: Darewych)

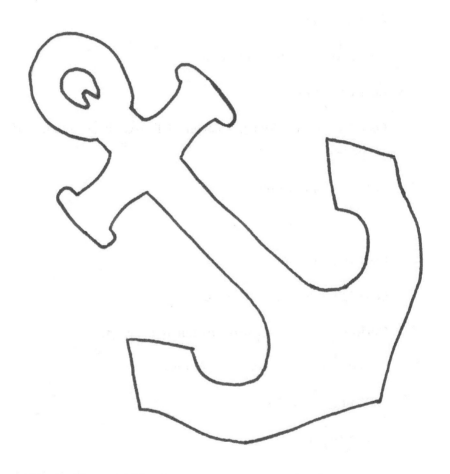

APPENDIX M: FUTURE TRIP DRAWING RATING SCALE (2017, revised 2018. Source: Darewych, 2017b)

Image characteristics/variables

1. **Axis of the paper:** Indicate the axis of the paper.

   Code 0 for horizontal axis

   Code 1 for vertical axis

   Code 2 for undefined.

2. **Symbol type:** Indicate the symbol depicted in the drawing.

   Code 0 for person

   Code 1 for place

   Code 2 for object

   Code 3 for multiple—person, place, and object.

3. **Placement of self in the picture:** Indicate if person depicts self in picture.

   Code 0 for no self

   Code 1 if self is depicted in picture.

4. **Written association tense:** Indicate the tense of the written association.

   Code 0 for past tense

   Code 1 for present tense

   Code 2 for future tense

   Code 3 for multiple tense.

APPENDIX N: BUS TO FUTURE ACTIVITY
SHEET (Source: Darewych and Zeller Cooper)

APPENDIX O: DOWNWARD AND UPWARD SPIRAL ACTIVITY SHEET

(Source: Kuzmich)

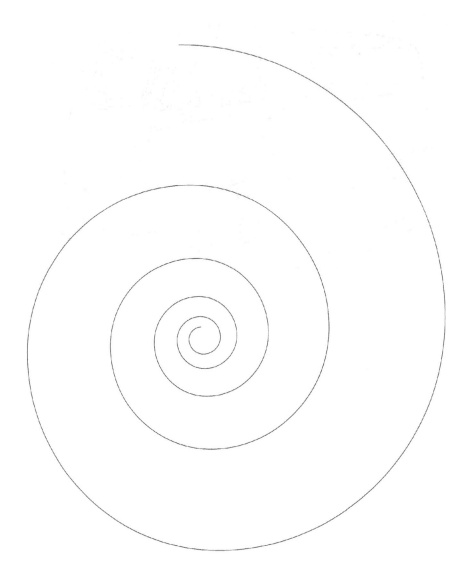

APPENDIX P: LIVING IN THE PRESENT— MARKETPLACE PHOTOGRAPH
(Source: Zeller Cooper, 2019)

APPENDIX Q: LIVING IN THE PRESENT—MARKETPLACE ACTIVITY SHEET (Source: Zeller Cooper, 2019)

©livinginthepresent.ca

APPENDIX R: LABYRINTH ACTIVITY SHEET (Source: Kuzmich)

References

Allen, P. (2005). *Art is a Spiritual Path*. Boston, MA: Shambhala Publications.

Babouchkina, A. & Robbins, S. J. (2015). "Reducing mood through mandala creation: A randomized controlled trial." *Art Therapy, 32*(1), 34–39.

Backer van Ommeren, T., Koot, H. M., Scheeren, A. M., & Begeer, S. (2015). "Reliability and validity of the interactive drawing test: A measure of reciprocity for children and adolescents with autism spectrum disorder." *Journal of Autism and Developmental Disorders, 45*(7), 1967–1977. doi:10.1007/s10803-014-2353-x.

Bannink, F. (2015). *Handbook of Positive Supervision: For Supervisors, Facilitators, and Peer Groups*. Boston, MA: Hagrefe.

Baumeister, R. & Vohs, K. (2004). *Handbook of Self-Regulation: Research, Theory, and Application*. New York, NY: Guilford Press.

Baumeister, R. & Vohs, K. (2010). "The Pursuit of Meaningfulness in Life." In C. Snyder (ed.), *Handbook of Positive Psychology* (pp.608–617). Oxford: Oxford University Press.

Butler, T. (2010). *Getting Unstuck: A Guide to Discovering Your Next Career Path*. Boston, MA: Harvard Business Press.

Cane, F. (1951). *The Artist in Each of Us*. Craftsbury Common, VT: Art Therapy.

Chilton, G. & Wilkinson, R. (2016). "Positive Art Therapy." In J. A. Rubin (ed.), *Approaches to Art Therapy: Theory and Technique* (third edition, pp.249–267). New York, NY: Routledge.

Chodorow, J. (1997). *Jung on Active Imagination.* London: Routledge.

Conner, T. S., DeYoung, C. G., & Silvia, P. J. (2016). "Everyday creative activity as a path to flourishing." *The Journal of Positive Psychology,* 1–9. doi:10.1080/17439760.2016.1257049.

Corey, G., Schneider Corey, M., Corey, C., & Callanan, P. (2015). *Issues and Ethics in the Helping Professions* (ninth edition). Belmont, CA: Brooks/ Cole.

Csikszentmihályi, M. (1991). *Flow: The Psychology of Optimal Experience.* New York, NY: Harper Perennial.

Csikszentmihályi, M. (1996). *Creativity: Flow and the Psychology of Discovery and Intervention.* New York, NY: HarperCollins Publishers.

Csikszentmihályi, M. (1997). *Finding Flow: The Psychology of Engagement with Everyday Life.* New York, NY: Basic Books.

da Silva, P. (2005). *Logoart: Searching Meaning Through Art.* Sao Paulo, Brazil: Edicoes Inteligentes.

Damon, W. (2009). *The Path to Purpose: How Young People Find their Calling in Life.* New York, NY: Free Press.

Darewych, O. H. (2013). "Building bridges with institutionalized orphans in Ukraine: An art therapy pilot study." *The Arts in Psychotherapy,* *40*(1), 85–93. doi:10.1016/j.aip.2012.10.1001.

Darewych, O. H. (2014). *The Bridge Drawing with Path Art-Based Assessment: Measuring Meaningful Life Pathways in Higher Education Students* (Doctoral dissertation). Available from ProQuest Dissertations and Theses database (UMI No. 3615961).

Darewych, O. H. (2017a) *Scribble drawing rating scale.* Unpublished rating scale.

Darewych, O. H. (2017b) *Future trip drawing scale.* Unpublished rating scale.

Darewych, O. H. (2019). "Positive Arts Interventions: Creative Tools Helping Mental Health Students Flourish." In L. E. van Zyl & S. Rothmann (eds), *Theoretical Approaches to Multi-Cultural Positive Psychological Interventions* (pp.431–444). Cham, Switzerland: Springer. doi.org/10.1007/978-3-030-20583-6_19.

Darewych, O. H. (in press). "Cultivating Psychological Well-Being through Arts-Based Interventions." In L. Tay & J. Pawelski (eds), *Handbook of Positive Psychology and the Arts and Humanities.* Oxford: Oxford University Press.

Darewych, O. H. & Brown Campbell, K. (2016). "Measuring future orientations and goals with the bridge drawing: A review of the global research." *Canadian Art Therapy Association Journal, 29*(1), 30–37. doi:10.1080/08322473.2016.1166010.

Darewych, O. H., Newton, N., & Farrugie, K. W. (2018). "Investigating imagination in adults with autism with art-based assessments." *Journal on Developmental Disabilities, 23*(2), 27–36.

Darewych, O. H., & Riedel Bowers, N. (2017). "Positive arts interventions: Creative clinical tools promoting psychological well-being." *International Journal of Art Therapy: Inscape, 23*(2), 62–69. doi:10.1 080/17454832.2017.1378241.

Denborough, D. (2008). *Collective Narrative Practice: Responding to Individuals, Groups, and Communities who have Experienced Trauma.* Adelaide: Dulwich Centre Publications.

Diener, E. & Chan, M. (2011). "Happy people live longer: Subjective well-being contributes to health and longevity." *Applied Psychology: Health and Well-being, 3,* 1–43.

Diener, E., Suh, E., Lucas, R., & Smith, H. (1999). "Subjective well-being: three decades of progress." *Psychological Bulletin, 125*(2), 276–302.

Diener, E., Wirtz, D., Tov, W., Kim-Prieto, C., *et al.* (2009). "New measures of well-being: Flourishing and positive and negative feelings." *Social Indicators Research, 97,* 247–266. doi:10.1007/s11205-009-9493-y.

Emmons, R. A. (2003). "Personal Goals, Life Meaning, and Virtue: Wellsprings of a Positive Life." In C. M. Keyes & J. Haidt (eds), *Flourishing: Positive Psychology and the Life Well-Lived* (pp.105–128). Washington, DC: American Psychological Association. doi:10.1037/10594-005.

Forgeard, M. J. C. & Eichner, K. V. (2014). "Creativity as a Target and Tool for Positive Interventions." In A. C. Parks & S. M. Schuller (eds), *Handbook of Positive Psychological Interventions* (pp.137–154). Oxford: Wiley-Blackwell.

Frankl, V. E. (1986). *The Doctor and the Soul* (second edition). New York, NY: Random House.

Frankl, V. E. (2006). *Man's Search for Meaning* (revised and updated). Boston, MA: Beacon Press (originally published 1946).

Fredrickson, B. L. (1998). "What good are positive emotions?" *Review of General Psychology, 2,* 300–319.

Fredrickson, B. L. (2009). *Positivity.* New York, NY: Three Rivers Press.

Fredrickson, B. L. & Losada, M. F. (2005). "Positive affect and the complex dynamics of human flourishing." *American Psychologist, 60,* 678–686. doi.org/10.1037/0003-066X.60.7.678.

Freudenberger, H. J. (1975). "The staff burn-out syndrome in alternative institutions." *Psychotherapy: Theory, Research, and Practice, 12,* 73–82.

Fuller, R. C. (2001). *Spiritual, but not Religious: Understanding Unchurched America.* New York, NY: Oxford University Press.

Griffith, J. L. & Griffith, M. E. (2002). *Encountering the Sacred in Psychotherapy: How to Talk with People about their Spiritual Lives.* New York, NY: Guilford Press.

Haslam, M. J. (1997). "Art therapy considered within the tradition of symbolic healing." *Canadian Art Therapy Association Journal, 11*(1), 2–16. doi:10.1080/08322473.1997.11432225.

Hays, R. & Lyon, S. (1981). "The bridge drawing: A projective technique for assessment in art therapy." *The Arts in Psychotherapy, 8*(4), 207–217.

Jackson, S. A. & Marsh, H. W. (1996). "Development and validation of a scale to measure optimal experience: The flow state scale." *Journal of Sport and Exercise Psychology, 18*(1), 17–35.

Jahoda, M. (1958). *Current Concepts of Positive Mental Health.* New York, NY: Basic Books.

Joseph, S. (2015). *Positive Therapy: Building Bridges between Positive Psychology and Person-Centred Psychotherapy* (second edition). New York, NY: Routledge.

Joseph, S. & Linley, P. A. (2004). *Positive Therapy: A Positive Psychology in Practice.* In P. A. Linley & S. Joseph (Eds) Positive Psychology in Practice (pp.354–368). Hoboken, NJ: Wiley.

Jung, R. E., Flores, R. A., & Hunter, D. (2016). "A new measure of imagination ability: Anatomical brain imaging correlates." *Frontiers in Psychology, 7*(496), 1–8.

Kast, V. (1992). *The Dynamics of Symbols: Fundamentals of Jungian Psychotherapy* (S. A. Schwarz, trans.). New York, NY: Fromm International.

Kaufman, J. C. & Beghetto, R. A. (2009). "Beyond big and little: The four c model of creativity." *Review of General Psychology, 13*(1), 1–12. doi:10.1037/a0013688.

Kaufman, S. B. (2014, July 1). *Imagination Institute to study how the mind conjures* [Web log post]. Retrieved from http://blogs.scientificamerican. com/beautiful-minds/imagination-institute-to-study-how-the-mind-conjures.

Koenig, H. G., McCullough, M. E., & Larson, D. B. (2001). *Handbook of Religion and Health.* Oxford: Oxford University Press.

Kramer, E. (1971). *Art as Therapy with Children.* New York, NY: Schocken Books.

Kurtz, J. L. & Lyubomirsky, S. (2013). "Happiness Promotion: Using Mindful Photography to Increase Positive Emotion and Appreciation." In J. J. Froh & A. C. Parks (eds), *Activities for Teaching Positive Psychology: A Guide for Instructors* (pp.133–136). Washington, DC: American Psychological Association. doi:10.1037/14042-021.

Landy, R. (1993). *Persona and Performance: The Meaning of Role in Drama, Therapy, and Everyday Life.* New York, NY: Guilford Press.

Lantz, J. (1993). "Art, logotherapy, and the unconscious god." *Journal of Religion and Health, 32*(3), 179–187.

Lazarus, R. S. (2003). "Does the positive psychology movement have legs?" *Psychological Inquiry, 14*, 93–109.

Lester, A. (2015). *On Multiple Selves.* New York, NY: Routledge.

Linley, A. (2008). *Average to A+: Realising Strengths in Yourself and Others.* Coventry: CAPP Press.

Locke, E. A. & Latham, G. P. (1990). *A Theory of Goal Setting & Task Performance.* Englewood Cliffs, NJ: Prentice-Hall.

Lomas, T. (2016). "Postive art: Artistic expression and appreciation as an exemplary vehicle for flourishing." *Review of General Psychology, 20*(2), 171–182. doi.org/10.1037/gpr0000073.

Lyubomirsky, S. & Layous, K. (2013). "How do simple positive activities increase well-being?" *Current Directions in Psychological Science, 22*(1), 57–62. doi:10.1177/0963721412469809.

Lyubomirsky, S. & Lepper, H. S. (1999). "A measure of subjective happiness: Preliminary reliability and construct validation." *Social Indicators Research, 46*, 137–155.

Malchiodi, C. A. (2002). *The Soul's Palette: Drawing on Art's Transformative Powers for Health and Well-Being.* Boston, MA: Shambhala.

Malchiodi, C. A. (ed.) (2005). *Expressive Therapies.* New York, NY: Guilford Press.

Malchiodi, C.A. (2007). *The Art Therapy Sourcebook* (second edition). New York, NY: McGraw-Hill.

Manning, T. M. (1987). "Aggression depicted in abused children's drawings." *The Arts in Psychotherapy, 14*(1), 15–24. doi:10.1016/0197-4556(87)90031-1.

Markus, H. & Nurius, P. (1986). "Possible selves." *American Psychologist, 41*, 954–969. doi:10.1037/003-066X.41.9.954.

Mascaro, N. & Rosen, D. H. (2006). "The role of existential meaning as a buffer against stress." *Journal of Humanistic Psychology, 46*, 168–190.

Maslow, A. H. (1970). *Motivation and Personality* (second edition). New York, NY: Harper & Row.

McConnell, A. R. (2011). "The multiple self-aspects framework: Self-concept representation and its implications." *Personality and Social Psychology Review, 15*(1), 3–27. doi:10.1177/1088868310371101.

McCullough, M. E., Emmons, R. A., & Tsang, J. (2002). "The grateful disposition: A conceptual and empirical topography." *Journal of Personality and Social Psychology, 82*, 112–127.

McNiff, S. (2009). *Integrating the Arts in Therapy: History, Theory, and Practice.* Springfield, IL: Charles C. Thomas. doi:10.1037/003-066X.41.9.954.

Niemiec, R. M. (2013). "VIA Character Strengths: Research and Practice (The First 10 Years)." In H. H. Knoop & A. Delle Fave (eds), *Well-Being and Cultures: Perspectives on Positive Psychology* (pp.11–30). New York, NY: Springer.

Niemiec, R. M. (2014). *Mindfulness and Character Strengths: A Practical Guide to Flourishing.* Cambridge, MA: Hogrefe.

Niemiec, R. M. (2018). *Character Strengths Interventions: A Field-Guide for Practitioners.* Boston, MA: Hogrefe.

Niemiec, R. M. & Wedding, D. (2008). *Positive Psychology at the Movies: Using Films to Build Virtues and Character Strengths.* Gottingen, Germany: Hogrefe & Huber.

O'Hanlon, B. & Bertolino, B. (2012). *The Therapist's Notebook on Positive Psychology: Activities, Exercises, and Handouts.* New York, NY: Routledge/Taylor & Francis Group.

Ortberg, J. & Barton, R. H. (2001). *An Ordinary Day with Jesus: Participant's Guide.* Barrington, IL: Willow Creek Association, 67–72.

Owens, R. L. & Patterson, M. M. (2013). "Positive psychological interventions for children: A comparison of gratitude and best possible selves approaches." *The Journal of Genetic Psychology, 174*(4), 403–428. doi:10.1080/00221325.2012.697496.

Pargament, K. I. (2007). *Spirtually Integrated Psychotherapy: Understanding and Addressing the Sacred.* New York, NY: Guilford Press.

Park, N. & Peterson, C. (2006). "Methodological Issues in Positive Psychology and the Assessment of Character Strengths." In A. D. Ong & M. van Dulmen (eds), *Handbook of Methods in Positive Psychology* (pp.292–305). New York, NY: Oxford University Press.

Park, N., Peterson, C., & Seligman, M. E. P. (2004). "Strengths of character and well-being." *Journal of Social and Clinical Psychology, 2*(5), 603–619.

Pelaprat, E. & Cole, M. (2011). "Minding the gap: Imagination, creativity, and human cognition." *Integrative Psychological and Behavioural Science, 45*(4), 397–418. doi:10.1007/s12124-011-9176-5.

Pennebaker, J. W. & Smyth, J. M. (2016). *Opening up by Writing it Down: How Expressive Writing Improves Health and Eases Emotional Pain* (third edition). New York, NY: Guilford Press.

Peterson, C., Park, N., Pole, N., D'Andrea, W., & Seligman, M. E. P. (2008). "Strengths of character and posttraumatic growth." *Journal of Traumatic Stress, 21*(2), 214–217.

Peterson, C. & Seligman, M. E. P. (2004). *Character Strengths and Virtues: A Handbook and Classification.* Washington, DC: American Psychological Association; New York, NY: Oxford University Press.

Plante, T. G. (2008). *Using Spiritual and Religious Tools in Psychotherapy.* Washington, DC: American Psychological Association.

Puig, A., Lee, S. L., Goodwin, L., & Sherrard, P. (2006). "The efficacy of creative arts therapies to enhance emotional expression, spirituality, and psychological well-being of newly diagnosed Stage I and Stage II breast cancer patients: A preliminary study." *The Arts in Psychotherapy, 33*(3), 218–228.

Rashid, T. (2008). "Positive Psychotherapy." In S. J. Lopez (ed.), *Positive Psychology: Exploring the Best in People* (Vol. IV, pp.188–217). Westport, CT: Praeger.

Rashid, T. (2015). "Positive psychotherapy: A strengths-based approach." *The Journal of Positive Psychology, 10*, 25–40.

Ravensdaughter (2016). *The Celtic Mandalynth Workbook: Mindful Tracing Art for Stress, Anxiety and Attention Management.* Crestline, California. Celtic Art Store.

Reynolds, F. & Prior, S. (2006). "Creative adventures and flow in art-making: A qualitative study of women living with cancer." *British Journal of Occupational Therapy, 69*(6), no pages.

Riedel Bowers, N. & Darewych, O. H. (2019). "Expressive Arts: Instruments for Individual and Community Change." In P. A. Dunn (ed.), *Holistic Healing: Theories, Practices, and Social Change* (pp.181–197). Toronto, CA: Canadian Scholars Press.

Rogers, C. R. (1951). *Client-Centered Therapy: Its Current Practice, Implications and Theory.* Boston, MA: Houghton-Mifflin.

Rubin, J. A. (1999). *Art Therapy: An Introduction.* Philadelphia, PA: Brunner/Mazel.

Ryff, C. D. (1989). "Happiness is everything, or is it? Explorations on the meaning of psychological well-being." *Journal of Personality and Social Psychology, 57*(6), 1069–1081. doi:10.1037/0022-3514.57.6.1069.

Ryff, C. D. & Keyes, C. L. M. (1995). "The structure of psychological well-being revisited." *Journal of Personality and Social Psychology, 69*(4), 719–727.

Schein, E. H. (1978). *Career Dynamics: Matching Individual and Organizational Needs.* Reading, MA: Addison-Wesley.

Seligman, M. E. P. (1999). "The president's address." *American Psychologist, 54,* 559–562.

Seligman, M. E. P. (2004). "Foreword." In P. A. Linley & S. Joseph (eds), *Positive Psychology in Practice* (pp.xi–xiii). Hoboken: Wiley.

Seligman, M. E. P. (2011). *Flourish: A Visionary New Understanding of Happiness and Well-Being.* New York, NY: Free Press.

Seligman, M. E. P. & Csikszentmihályi, M. (2000). "Positive psychology: An introduction." *American Psychologist, 55*(1), 5–14. doi:10.1037/0003-066X.55.1.5.

Seligman, M. E. P., Ernst, R. M., Gillham, J., Reivich, K., & Linkins, M. (2009). "Positive education: Positive psychology and classroom interventions." *Oxford Review of Education, 35*(2), 293–311. doi:10.1080/03054980902934563.

Seligman, M. E. P., Steen, T. A., Park, N., & Peterson, C. (2005). "Positive psychology progress: Empirical validation of interventions." *American Psychologist, 60,* 410–421.

Shim, Y., Tay, L., Ward, M., & Pawelski, J. O. (2019). "Arts and humanities engagement: An integrative conceptual framework for psychological research." *Review of General Psychology, 23*(2), 159–176.

Simonton, D. K. (2000). "Creativity: Cognitive, developmental, personal, and social aspects." *American Psychologist, 55,* 151–158.

Snyder, C. R., Sympson, S. C., Ybasco, F. C., Borders, T. F., Babyak, M. A., & Higgins, R. L. (1996). "Development and validation of the State Hope Scale." *Journal of Personality and Social Psychology, 70,* 321–335.

Steger, M. F. (2012). "Experiencing Meaning in Life: Optimal Functioning at the Nexus of Well-Being, Psychopathology, and Spirituality." In P. T. P. Wong (ed.), *The Human Quest for Meaning: A Handbook of Psychological Research and Clinical Applications* (second edition, pp.165–184). Mahwah, NJ: Erlbaum.

Steger, M. F., Frazier, P., Oishi, S., & Kaler, M. (2006). "The meaning in life questionnaire: Assessing the presence of and search for meaning in life." *Journal of Counseling Psychology, 53*(1), 80–93.

Steger, M. F., Kashdan, T. B., Sullivan, B. A., & Lorentz, D. (2008). "Understanding the search for meaning in life: Personality, cognitive style, and the dynamic between seeking and experiencing meaning." *Journal of Personality, 76,* 199–228.

Steger, M. F., Shim, Y., Rush, B. R., Brueske, R. A., Shin, J. Y., & Merriman, L. A. (2013). "The mind's eye: A photographic method for understanding meaning in people's lives." *The Journal of Positive Psychology, 8*(6), 530–542. doi:10.1080/17439760.2013.830760.

Tay, L., Pawelski, J. O., & Keith, M. G. (2017). "The role of the arts and humanities in human flourishing: A conceptual model." *Journal of Positive Psychology, 13*(3), 215–225. doi.org/10.1080/17439760.2017.1279207.

Tomasulo, D. J. (2018, August 15). *Strengths atom* [Web log post]. Retrieved from www.ippanetwork.org/2018/08/15/strengths-atom.

Tomasulo, D. J. (2019). "The Virtual Gratitude Visit (VGV): Using Psychodrama and Role-Playing as a Positive Intervention." In L. E. van Zyl & S. Rothmann (eds), *Positive Psychological Intervention Design and Protocols for Multi-Cultural Contexts* (pp.405–413). Switzerland: Springer. doi.org/10.1007/978-3-030-20020-6_18.

Turner, J. H. (2000). *On the Origins of Human Emotions: A Sociological Inquiry into the Evolution of Human Affect.* Palo Alto, CA: Stanford University Press.

Vaish, A., Grossmann, T., & Woodward, A. (2008). "Not all emotions are created equal: The negativity bias in social-emotional development." *Psychological Bulletin, 134*(3), 383–403. doi:10.1037/0033-2909.134.3.383.

Vallerand, R. J. (2013). *The Psychology of Passion: A Dualistic Model.* New York, NY: Oxford University Press.

Weiss, L. (2004). *Therapist's Guide to Self-Care.* New York, NY: Routledge.

Wilkinson, R. A. & Chilton, G. (2013). "Positive art therapy: Linking positive psychology to art therapy theory, practice, and research." *Art Therapy: Journal of the American Art Therapy Association, 30*(1), 4–11.

Wilkinson, R. A. & Chilton, G. (2018). *Positive Art Therapy Theory and Practice: Integrating Positive Psychology with Art Therapy.* New York, NY: Routledge.

Wong, P. T. P. (2012). "From Logotherapy to Meaning-Centered Counseling and Therapy." In P. T. P. Wong (ed.), *The Human Quest for Meaning: A Handbook of Psychological Research and Clinical Applications* (second edition, pp.619–647). Mahwah, NJ: Erlbaum.

Worthington, E. L., Jr. (2001). *Five Steps to Forgiveness: The Art and Science of Forgiving*. New York, NY: Crown.

Zeller Cooper, E. (2019). *Living in the Present*. Retrieved from https://livinginthepresent.ca.

Websites

British Art Therapy Association: www.baat.org

Canadian Art Therapy Association: www.canadianarttherapy.org

Canadian Positive Psychology Association:
www.positivepsychologycanada.com

Celtic Art Therapy: www.celticarttherapy.com

Creative Wellbeing Workshops: www.creativewellbeingworkshops.com

Dan Tomasulo's Virtual Gratitude Visit:
www.youtube.com/watch?v= izGmSvOmYXc

Esther Zeller Cooper's Living in the Present: www.livinginthepresent.ca

European Network for Positive Psychology: http://enpp.eu

Humanities and Human Flourishing Project:
www.humanitiesandhumanflourishing.org

The Imagination Institute: www.imagination-institute.org

International Expressive Arts Therapy Association: www.ieata.org

International Network on Personal Meaning: www.meaning.ca

International Positive Psychology Association: www.ippanetwork.org

Positive Psychology Center: www.ppc.sas.upenn.edu

Positive Psychology Questionnaires: www.authentichappiness.org

Resources on Character Strengths: www.viacharacter.org

VIA Institute on Character: www.viacharacter.org

VIA Survey of Character Strengths (free, online): www.viame.org

Biography

Olena Darewych PhD, RP, RCAT is a registered psychotherapist in Ontario, a registered Canadian art therapist, an adjunct faculty at Adler University, Vancouver campus, and Martin Luther University College/ Wilfrid Laurier University, and instructor at the Toronto Art Therapy Institute (TATI). She completed her PhD in expressive therapies at Lesley University and has facilitated art therapy workshops and training nationally and internationally. As a mental health practitioner, she has 19 years of experience working with individuals of all ages and from culturally diverse backgrounds in a variety of community settings in Australia, Canada, the USA, and Ukraine. She currently facilitates group digital art therapy sessions for adults with autism spectrum disorder and other developmental disabilities. As an educator, she designs and implements hands-on experiential courses wherein students undergo self-discovery and learn through the arts. She is a Past President of the Canadian Art Therapy Association and a member of the Canadian Positive Psychology Association.

Subject Index

Author Index

206

POSITIVE PSYCHOLOGY ARTS ACTIVITIES